THE SILENT REVOLUTION

Muhammad A. Faour

Muhammad Faour is an Associate Professor of Sociology and the Chairperson of the Department of Social and Behavioral Sciences at the American University of Beirut. He is the author of *The Arab World after Desert Storm* (1993), *Operations Research in Family Planning in Lebanon* (1996), and co-author of *University Students in Lebanon, Background and Attitudes* (1998, in Arabic). His work includes a number of English and Arabic articles on subjects such as demography, family, and conflict management. Professor Faour has received a number of awards, notably, the Peace Fellow Award from the United States Institute of Peace and the Fulbright Research Award for Senior Scholars.

THE SILENT REVOLUTION IN LEBANON:
CHANGING VALUES OF THE YOUTH

BY MUHAMMAD FAOUR

AMERICAN UNIVERSITY OF BEIRUT

American University of Beirut, Beirut, Lebanon

To my wife Basma
With love and appreciation

TABLE OF CONTENTS

FIGURES

TABLES

6. Family Norms: Persistence and Change

7. Political Attitudes and Norms

ACKNOWLEDGEMENTS

The idea of this book was born after I conducted a number of opinion surveys of students at the American University of Beirut. This idea was translated into a research proposal on "Changing Social Norms among Women and Youth in Postwar Lebanon," which the Fulbright Program for Senior Scholars graciously accepted to support. The Fulbright award offered me the opportunity to analyze the data that I had collected and write the first draft of this book during my stay at Georgetown University between February and September of 1997. Many thanks to the Council for International Exchange of Scholars (CIES), which administers the Fulbright program, particularly to Program Officer Anita Kaplan, for her sincere help, moral support, and friendliness.

I am extremely grateful to Georgetown Professor Halim Barakat for his continuous encouragement, valuable comments, and exemplary friendly assistance throughout my stay in Washington, D.C. To me, Halim and his wife Hayat were the best example of Lebanese and Arab hospitality. Thanks are also due to the Center for Contemporary Arab Studies at Georgetown University, which provided me with office space and moral support.

Special thanks to Najwa Yahfoufi, Professor of Social Psychology at the Lebanese University, who worked meticulously to ensure that the respondents at the Lebanese University satisfactorily completed the questionnaire. In more ways than one, she was a real collaborator in this research. I acknowledge the serious work done by all my students who participated in collecting the data at AUB. Their enthusiasm about the survey was remarkable.

I also owe many thanks to the two external reviewers of the first draft for their useful comments and for strongly recommending the manuscript for publication. I tried to incorporate almost all of their suggestions, as well as those of Munir Bashshur, Chairman of AUB's publications committee. To him, I also extend special thanks for his comments and prompt response to my queries. I am grateful to Anissa Rafeh, the copy editor at the AUB publication's office, for doing a fine job in a short time, and to my graduate assistant Shereen Diab for preparing the index. Special thanks to my talented niece Dina Faour for designing the book cover.

Finally, I am more than grateful to my wife Basma for her intellectual insights, bright ideas, and everlasting love, and to our two children for tolerating my long stay away from them and for offering me the warm support and love that I needed during the preparation of the manuscript.

CHAPTER 1

INTRODUCTION

> We the youth have tomorrow.
> With its everlasting glory, we the youth.
> Our motto shall always be:
> Long live the homeland; long live the homeland.
> To it, our souls we donated during trying times.
>
> al-Akhtal al-Saghir[1]

Youth have repeatedly played an important role in maintaining the sociocultural dynamics of society.[2] Nations across the globe have relied "heavily on youth as the backbone of society."[3] The youth have often been viewed as the bedrock of social change and a driving force for revolutions. In Europe and the United States, the student rebellion of the 1960s engendered a series of radical shifts in political practices and social norms, albeit without fomenting popular upheavals or storming the "Bastilles" of established democracies. In developing countries, such as China, Latin America, Africa, and Southeast Asia, students were more radical, pursuing revolutionary political goals.

Lebanon is no exception, and is perhaps a good example of the role of youth, particularly college students, in social change. In many schools, Lebanese children and youth are socialized to see themselves as the future elite whose prospective role is crucial for the survival and prosperity of the nation. Singing "We the youth have tomorrow"[4] must have resonated loudly in the ears of many students, but foremost the political activists of the early 1970s.

The student movement that was active on the eve of the civil strife in the mid-70s was far more radical and influential than its

European and American analogues of the 1960s.   Undoubtedly, the students' actions, regardless of the movement's real objectives, rocked society's boat rather vigorously. From the ranks of the student movement rose radical chiefs for the emerging warring militias that plunged the country into a bloodbath for over fifteen years.[5] When the guns fell silent, some of those warlords maintained pivotal roles in the current political regime.[6] The role of the student movement during the war renders the study of Lebanese students' attitudes and norms a worthwhile endeavor. Not only would knowledge of their normative patterns enlighten us to their probable ensuing behavior, but it could also shed light on the nature of social change in the entire Lebanese society.

In addition to being a distinctive social category, students at high schools and colleges have been widely used in studies of norms and values. Unlike other social groups, students are conveniently available and are quite accessible to researchers for observation and questioning. Moreover, the academic setting renders students more receptive to social investigation than other categories of society. This is partly due to the nature of academia, which promotes scientific research.

Demographically, Lebanese college students belong to the 17-24 year old age group.   This age cohort comprises 16% of the total population, up from 13% in 1970.[7] Today, about one in six Lebanese belongs to that age group. This proportion is projected to increase slightly over the coming decade since the younger cohort of 10-14 year olds is larger in size than the cohort of 15-19 year olds, which in turn is larger than the cohort of 20-24 year olds.[8] The number of students in colleges and universities is about 90,000, or 18% of the population aged 17-24. This proportion is also expected to increase as the numbers of students in academic and technical colleges, particularly females, continue to rise. The trend toward increased enrollment in schools of higher learning is partly due to an increase in the number of these institutions as well as a growing public preference for higher education.

During the years of turmoil, 1975-1990, Lebanese youth had a unique, albeit painful, wartime experience. Unlike the youth in other countries, they spent the larger part of their childhood deprived of the pleasant joyful experiences of a child's world. They missed out on frequent family outings, going to school on a regular basis, playing with peers every day, sleeping in one's own bed, and more generally, having a peaceful, safe, and healthy environment. The endless nights of horrifying sounds of shelling and explosions turned their sweet dreams into ghastly nightmares.

In addition, many youths were personally affected by the acts of war. Data on Lebanese students at the American University of Beirut (AUB) show that most of them have experienced some form of atrocity. About 40% of AUB students witnessed the death of family members or friends, and more had family members or friends injured by bombs, bullets, or shrapnel. A large proportion of students (43%) cited damage to their family property. Many reported cases involving the kidnapping of kin or friends. Close to half of the students (46%) were involuntarily displaced from their homes for more than six months. Some students were kidnapped by militia groups hostile to their religious sects. Others were injured during the countless battles that shattered the country. Only a small minority—16%—escaped these horrendous events of war; some were out of the country when battles began; others lived in places that were virtually unscathed by the war.

When life returned to normal, Lebanese students were confronted with new realities in their country: visible alterations in social organization, as well as in political and economic systems. Life on the street, at college, and at home was different, and they had to adjust. Other changes had also appeared on the world scene—mainly in the world's political and economic order and that of the region as well. With the demise of the Soviet Union, the cold war was over. After the defeat of Iraq in Desert Storm, the Arab world became more atomized, under the burden of new economic and political problems. These factors, along with the personal war experience of students and the societal changes that occurred in the wake of the war, are all likely to have affected the students' perspectives on life, the nature of their relations with family members and friends, their political attitudes, norms, and self-perceptions.

However, little effort, if any, has been made to investigate such changes in the social norms and values. Most government plans for reconstructing war-ravished Lebanon focused on rebuilding and rehabilitating the country's physical infrastructure, a vital goal indeed. However, few plans dealt with certain aspects of the nation's human resources.[9] Therefore, it is no wonder that critics of postwar efforts have brandished government plans as aiming to "rebuild stones not souls."

An examination of social values and norms is essentially a study of culture for they both comprise its core. Social values refer to abstract beliefs about preferable or desirable behavior while norms are concrete rules of conduct. Values help in boosting the self-esteem of individuals and influence their social and political attitudes toward such issues as race, gender, class, and family. Likewise, social norms play a critical role in an individual's life; or as put by sociologist Talcott Parsons, social action is influenced by institutionalized norms.[10] Some psychologists assert that norms have a significant effect on collective action.[11] Postmodernist Habermas defines a community as "the structured set of norms and institutions."[12]

The study of norms and values in a postwar setting falls neatly within the domain of social change. Social change refers to the transformation in the social, economic, and political systems of society. Well before the emergence of modern sociology as a discipline, the subject of social change had occupied the minds and hearts of social scientists for centuries. For example, the *Muqaddima* of the medieval Arab scholar Ibn Khaldun comprises a treatise on social change. Masters of contemporary sociological thought belabored to comprehend and predict social change. From Comte, the founder of Western sociology, to Spencer, Durkheim, Tonnies, Marx, Weber, Parsons, and today's postmodern theorists, the interest in social change has continued unabated. In this study, social change is hypothesized to impinge on the normative structure.

The relation between culture, or values and norms, on the one hand, and social structure on the other, has been the subject of a long-standing debate among sociologists. This author neither endorses the classical Marxian thesis that infrastructure or mode of production determines superstructure to which values and norms belong, nor adopts the extreme opposite viewpoint that culture determines infrastructure.[13] Rather, both culture and structure are viewed as equally important and dialectically related. Furthermore, the individual plays an innovative, effective role in influencing both. Old norms affect social structure, and altered social structure can change old norms. Both a "sociocultural lifeworld" and a "social system," Habermas argues, characterize society.[14] Together with action, ideas have a "reflexive, transformative power."[15]

There are interconnections between various aspects of the social system—the economy, polity, culture, social organization, and daily interaction. These interconnections are not satisfactorily portrayed in any single theoretical perspective. Given that, this study has incorporated an eclectic, "multiperspectival" approach. Included in this approach are the agent-structure dualism, Giddens' notions of "production" and "reproduction" of social life and relations of power and inequality, Bourdieu's concept of "habitus," and Habermas's concept of "lifeworld" and his view of the social role of ideas and norms. Norms and values are significant determinants of behavior in a society that is characterized by power relations and conflict. But power, in my opinion, is more diffuse than was envisioned by Marx.[16]

The nature of the study population, i.e. youth taken as a collective, and the interest in social change as a macro phenomenon shifts the emphasis of the study approach to the macro features of society. The micro aspects of youth such as characteristics of their daily face-to-face social interaction and intimate personal life are beyond the scope of this work, though by no means insignificant as sociological phenomena.

Objectives of the Study

The aim of the study is to investigate the prevalence of a set of social values and norms among Lebanese college students, then compare, where feasible, the results with relevant pre-war data. The set includes individual values, societal values, family norms, and political norms.

Since these attitudes, norms, and values are influenced by such personal attributes as gender, religious affiliation, social class, academic institution, college major, religiosity, and ideological orientation, the impact of these factors will also be examined. For a better understanding of the value orientations and normative patterns, they are placed within their sociological and historical contexts. In employing this approach, the study takes into account the changing and persistent characteristics of the Lebanese society, which was subjected to various domestic and external influences. These influences include a long devastating civil war, a new regional political system, a new world order, and different local demographic, economic and political conditions.

The postwar data are drawn from sample surveys of Lebanese students aged 17-24 years at the American University of Beirut (hereafter referred to as AUB) and the Lebanese University (hereafter referred to as LU).

AUB is an American-run institution that follows the U.S. curriculum and criteria of admission and evaluation. It has a single campus located in West Beirut. AUB is highly competitive, thus admitting the best students from the various districts of Lebanon and from other Arab countries. Its tuition fees are relatively high by Lebanese standards, which would make most lower class students hesitant to apply unless they can secure a scholarship or loan from some source.   AUB, however, provides considerable financial aid to qualified, needy students after they are admitted.

The Lebanese University is the sole public university in the country. It is also the largest in terms of student enrollment and number of faculty members.   LU students of both sexes belong to the various religious communities; they come from both urban and rural areas, from all districts of Lebanon, and have a diversity of social-class backgrounds. However, most have lower or lower-middle class backgrounds since the university is essentially tuition-free, and its academic standard does not measure up to the standards of the top private universities.   For that reason, it is easier for students to be admitted to LU than to other universities.   As for the LU curriculum, it is heavily influenced by the curricula prevailing in French universities since most of its faculty and administration are French-trained.   LU has branches in all the *muhafazat,* or provinces, and in both the largely Christian part of Beirut and the largely Muslim part.   Both branches and various faculties in Greater Beirut were included in the survey population.

By covering AUB and LU students, the study covers the normative patterns of Lebanese students reasonably well.   Three other major universities were not included for lack of funds: Lebanese American University (LAU, formerly BUC), Beirut Arab University (BAU), and Saint Joseph University (USJ).   LAU, which follows an American curriculum, attracts students who have similar educational and social backgrounds to those at AUB, thus, the exclusion of LAU is not expected to affect the nature of the study results.   BAU, an Egyptian-run university affiliated with Alexandria University, attracts students who come from social and educational backgrounds that are close to those who attend LU.   However, the religious composition of BAU students is tilted more heavily toward Muslims.   As for USJ, most of its students are Christians belonging to middle and upper social classes.   By taking account of social class and religious affiliation in the data analysis, the study findings may become generalizable to all Lebanese university students.

The pre-war comparable quantitative data are primarily from a study of college students by Halim Barakat.[17]   Three other pre-war studies that have very few comparable data are also used.   The first is by Diab and Melikian,[18] the second by Nasr and Palmer,[19] and the third by Theodor

Hanf.[20] There are no other known reliable data before 1975; however, there are several studies that dealt with one or more of the issues discussed in this book.   Some of these studies used a subjective judgmental approach while others based their findings on observations by the authors or selected informants. A selected number of these studies are utilized because they provide useful background on the traditional values and norms that were characteristic of students or Lebanese society before 1975. In comparing the current data with that of the pre-war years, similarities and differences between the two sets of data are pointed out. In addition, the study examines some determinants of the normative patterns and discusses implications of the findings for both future academic research and policy considerations.

The findings reveal impressive changes in the social values and norms of Lebanese college students. There is strong evidence of a rise in democratic practices within the nuclear family. One indicator is the increasing participation of mothers in making decisions about important issues relating to their families. Another indicator is the prevalence of equalitarian social norms among students. A third indicator is the low level of the individual value of authoritarianism among students and the high level of individualism.

A silent, normative revolution appears to be taking place among the Lebanese youth. As shall be argued later in the book, this revolution has far-reaching implications for the Lebanese society as a whole for it reflects normative changes in the family, the most crucial social institution in Arab societies.

Organization of the Book

The first logical step in this endeavor is to define each of the concepts employed in the study, namely, attitudes, norms, values, and change. Chapter 2 reviews the diversity of definitions of norms and values to reveal the complexity of these concepts and their controversial nature. The theoretical relevance of norms and values to social action and change is highlighted, and a number of empirical studies are cited. Chapter 3 examines previous research conducted on this topic, with special emphasis on Lebanon, and describes the methodology of the study, its data, and the background characteristics for the respondents—including gender, major, religious sect, place of residence, and educational level and occupation of parents.

Chapter 4 provides a brief overview of the changes in the social structure. It is this author's judgment that these changes have taken place since the early seventies, shortly before the civil war commenced. This should serve as a useful backdrop for interpreting the empirical findings on students' attitudes and value orientations. Which aspects of Lebanon's social structure, if any, have changed, and which have persisted over the past three decades? The chapter attempts to answer this question at the macro-level by examining change and stability in the demography, economy, political system, and social organization. It assembles a combination of recent macro-data, personal observations, qualitative studies, and journalistic reports. Relevant studies dating back to the pre-war years are used as a baseline for comparison.

Chapter 5 investigates the prevalence of a set of individual values such as authoritarianism, individualism, and equalitarianism. These personal values may reflect certain societal values, which in turn explain several themes and observations presented in chapter 4. The data are analyzed further by considering socioeconomic and political determinants, correlates, and likely consequences of the students' values.

Chapter 6 identifies the three social groups, or categories, to which the students feel most closely attached. Temporal trends and socioeconomic differences in group-affiliations are investigated. Findings of studies conducted before 1975 are used for comparison. Since the nuclear family is found to be the social group with which the large majority of students identify most, the nature of relations within the family are discussed at some length. The chapter covers issues of authority, obedience, love, and disputes within the Lebanese family, as portrayed by AUB students. Not only are general patterns discerned, but also variations by social class, level of education of parents, religious affiliation, and degree of religiosity. The data are linked with themes and ideas from earlier chapters. Some of the findings on family issues and group affiliations are explained in terms of specified individual values.

Chapter 7 presents students' political perceptions and norms, as revealed by the survey responses. The perceptions relate to sectarianism, identification of most liked and most disliked political leaders, nature of students' group identities, political orientations, their assessment of the country's economic, political, and social problems, and their future outlook. The analysis builds on these findings to examine variations of these attitudes and norms by such factors as gender and religious affiliation. This is followed by an interpretation of the data by linking them with themes and ideas from chapters 2 and 4.

Chapter 8 summarizes the main findings of the study and discusses their theoretical and practical significance. The chapter examines some of the broad implications of the findings for policy making in Lebanon, concluding with specific practical suggestions for the Lebanese government and other concerned social institutions.

Finally, the book has two appendices. Appendix A includes an analysis of variance (ANOVA) tables and results of the logistic regression analysis applied to a number of social and political values. The purpose of placing these statistical tables in the appendix is to simplify the presentation of empirical findings and avoid overwhelming those readers outside the academic community with advanced statistical techniques. In this appendix, the reader also finds two tables of detailed statistics from which table 7.13 was drawn. Appendix B includes the four survey questionnaires comprising the study's data set.

CHAPTER 2

VALUES, NORMS, AND CHANGE: A SOCIOLOGICAL PERSPECTIVE

> For very long and very short time spans, and from very deep and very shallow perspectives, things seem to be determined, but from the vast intermediate zone things seem to be a matter of free will. We can always shift our viewing angle to obtain the evidence of determinism or free will that we want.
>
> Immanuel Wallerstein[1]

Employed in this research are three basic sociological concepts: social values, norms, and change. The term "social" refers to a broad category that covers social, political, and economic aspects. Although the approach used in this study is sociological, other perspectives are also considered, notably, the psychological. The primary reason for emphasizing the sociological approach is this author's academic training in sociology. Another important reason, which could also be related to the first, is the contention that the research issues and questions posed in the first chapter will be more satisfactorily examined from a sociological viewpoint rather than a psychological, economic, or political viewpoint. The issues under investigation fall more neatly within the domain of sociology than other domains. Notably, the impact of social structure on norms can only be investigated within the turf of sociology. Nonetheless, it is deemed useful to utilize non-sociological approaches to understand certain aspects of the research problems.

Each of the three aforementioned concepts is examined separately. Diversified definitions and conceptions are provided to reveal the complexity of these concepts and their controversial nature. To underscore the practical relevance of values and norms, particularly with respect to social action, reference is made to a number of studies that examined their relationship with social behavior. The interrelation between norms and values as the core of culture on the one hand, and social structure and social change on the other hand, is then expounded. Since gender is a key concept for comprehending social behavior, the relation between gender, values, and social structure is discussed in a separate section.

Human Values: A Conception

Psychology and sociology textbooks are laden with definitions of the term "value". Social scientists have formulated a plethora of diverse, sometimes contradictory definitions, an indication that "value" is not a simple, easily defined term.

One psychologist, Norman Feather, refers to values as motives or frames of reference that form an integral part of the self-concept.[2] Seymour Epstein, another psychologist, objects to equating values with motives. He regards values as "beliefs about desirability that organize experience and direct behavior with respect to certain broad classes of events" while motives, such as aggression and sex, are more narrowly defined.[3] Other psychologists consider values to be preferred modes of conduct.[4]

Functionalist sociologists, beginning with their prominent leader Parsons, opposed the behaviorists' view that social values emerge in response to external stimuli. Instead, functionalists regard values as organizers of an individual's behavior in accordance with cognitive preferences. Not only do individuals have values, societies have them also. Values of societies, functionalists add, serve to balance citizens' needs as individuals with those of the larger society.[5] Parsons acknowledges that values and interests are linked: "Beliefs and values are actualized, partially and imperfectly, in realistic situations of social interaction and the outcomes are always codetermined by the values and the realistic exigencies."[6] However, in various other writings, Parsons clearly indicates that "values" have a primacy over "interests."

Clyde Kluckholn, another functionalist, defines a value as "a conception, explicit or implicit, distinctive of an individual or characteristic of a group, of the desirable, which influences the selection from available modes, means, and ends of action."[7] Kluckholn, Parsons, and Shils developed the notion of "value orientations" which are value systems that characterize a given society.[8]

European researchers, mostly sociologists, who undertook the comparative, large-scale Value Systems Study in 1990, employ a different definition. They describe a value that is held by an individual as "a disposition, a propensity to act in a certain way."[9] They use this same definition for values, beliefs, and attitudes. They consider all three to be "theoretical constructs" that are "not directly observable," but which can be utilized to "explain observable behavior."[10]

Building on the functionalists' work, particularly that of Parsons and Kluckholn, Milton Rokeach, a pioneer psychologist in the study of values, came up with the following definition:

> A value is an enduring belief that a specific mode of conduct or end-state of existence is personally or socially preferable to an opposite or converse mode of conduct or end-state of existence. A value system is an enduring organization of beliefs concerning desirable modes of conduct or end-states of existence along a continuum of relative importance.[11]

In his conception of value, Rokeach introduces the new idea that values involve a choice-based cognition, such as a preference of equality to justice. In line with these conceptions, sociologist Robin Williams refers to values as a host of orientations—including interests, preferences, duties, and goals—but, "the core phenomenon is the presence of criteria or standards of preference."[12] Values, as elaborated by Williams, incorporate three basic aspects: "cognitive, affective, and directional."[13] They are abstract and thus are not amenable to direct measurement by scientific methods.

Based on Rokeach's conception of value, this study defines a value as an enduring perception of preferred or desired social behavior or goal. It is by no means restricted to morality (such as the value of honesty or virtue), but covers various dimensions of human life.[14] Besides its conceptual appeal, Rokeach's definition of value has been widely employed in empirical studies across the globe. Most relevant to this work are comparative studies of pairs of Arab societies such as the comparison of values of Egyptian and Kuwaiti students, Egyptian and Saudi students, or Egyptian and Qatari adolescents.[15]

Values and behavior are related. Rokeach points to the role of values in enhancing one's self-esteem by offering standards of reference with regard to one's morality and various other social attitudes.[16] A number of empirical studies also show a significant association between values on the one hand, social behavior and attitudes such as racism, sexism, choice of friends, and political orientation, on the other.[17]

Human values may be classified in more ways than one. For example, corresponding to the "expressive" and "instrumental" types of action, Parsons proposes five pairs of value orientations that underlie all possible fundamental decisions:

Expressive	**Instrumental**
Affectivity	affective neutrality
Collectivity-orientation	self-orientation
Particularism	universalism
Diffuseness	specificity
Ascription	achievement[18]

The expressive type of action is typical of traditional societies whereas the instrumental type is typical of modern societies. For example, affectivity is present in family and friendship relationships that are characterized by emotions and intimacy. Affective neutrality exists in business-type relationships such as that between salesperson and client. Collectivity orientation denotes primacy of community over personal interests while self-oriented individuals give priority to their self-interests rather than the public good. Parsons contends that both individuals and societies can be classified according to this scheme, suggesting up to thirty-two "meaningful" combinations of these value-orientations or "pattern variables."[19]

The broadest general categorization divides human values into two main types: individual and societal. The former refers to values held by individual persons while the latter to common values shared by social groups, communities, or nations. In this study, individual as well as societal values are examined. The individual values include individualism or self-orientation, as opposed to collectivism, authoritarianism or extent of obedience to authority, equalitarianism, religiosity, fatalism, and degree of control over one's actions. Societal values, such as tribal solidarity, shame versus guilt, and form versus content, refer to stereotypic orientations of Arab societies, including Lebanon.

Social Norms: A Conception

Values are not the only component of normative systems that characterize all social groups; there is another vital component, namely, norms. Unlike values that are abstract, norms are concrete. Norms depend on values to provide them with "legitimation, boundary-setting... and linkage to other norms."[20] Although the concept of norms may seem simpler than that of value, the literature abounds with a variety of formal definitions by noted scholars. Some of these definitions, Robert Meier tells us, are not clear and rather confusing, while others are of little use for empirical research.[21]

William Goode, a sociologist, refers to norms as "specific sets of rules or definitions of proper behavior,"[22] a definition that is not quite useful although not incorrect. Sociologist Robert Nisbet, in his widely read text, *The Social Bond,* provides a confusing definition: norms are "adjustments, adaptations, so to speak, that human beings in interaction make to the surrounding environment...."[23] Even the famous sociologist Robert Merton, in his theory of deviance, does not define norms; he only states that anomie has a normative basis.

Social norms are defined in this book as "group-supported definitions of expected behavior in specific situations. These normative expectations are definitions of right and wrong, standards of conduct, rules and regulations."[24] Furthermore, norms "proscribe or prescribe" socially desirable behavior; when behavior is characterized by a normative pattern, it becomes a custom.[25]

Just like values, social norms play a critical role in one's life. Rational choice theories consider norms as determinants of an individual's choices.[26] Parsons has a different position. Citing Durkheim, he argues that social action is influenced by institutionalized norms that cannot be explained in terms of rational action.[27] Parsons portrays people as docile assimilators of norms and roles that are passed on to them through the process of socialization.[28] In Marxian thought, prevalent social values and norms play a powerful societal role in that they comprise part of the ideology of dominant classes. Marx points to the ability of ruling groups to justify their exploitation and power through their religious and political ideas that delude subordinate groups. Jon Elster, a psychologist, asserts that norms have a significant effect on collective action.[29]

Postmodernists also highlight the central role of norms in society and human interaction. Habermas, for example, defines a community as "the structured set of norms and institutions.... With every sequence of interaction, communication actors renew the appearance of a normatively structured society."[30] He distinguishes "purposive-rational action" that is based on technical rules from "communicative action." The latter refers to social interaction and is "governed by binding consensual norms which define reciprocal expectations about behavior and which must be understood and recognized by at least two acting subjects."[31] Purposive-rational action prevails in the state and the economy while communicative action dominates the family. Violation of technical rules results in failure to achieve designated objectives while the social community punishes the violation of consensual norms.

Social norms are recognized in at least two ways: by inference and reporting of appropriate action. The inferential strategy is to detect norms once they are violated. For instance, the norm of the right to property is discovered when one's property is stolen. In the reporting method, respondents are asked what individuals in their society/community should do in particular situations.[32] This is the method employed in this study in order to evaluate norms in Lebanon. Norms and values are relative; each varies in importance to its holder— be it an individual or collectivity—according to such factors as social class, gender, extent of exposure to the international system of communication, and extent of religiosity.[33]

In this book, social norms include political and family norms. Political norms deal with political orientations of students, sectarianism, and coexistence of religious groups. Family norms comprise love and respect for parents, the modesty code for women, democratic relations within the family, gender equity, and gender stereotypes.

Although there may be a gap between actual behavior and expected behavior that norms tap, the correlation between the two types of behavior in most stable societies is high. This correlation holds in Lebanon despite its political instability during the years 1975-1989 because the Lebanese society has sustained the basic features of its social organization. Religion and family are two basic social institutions of

Lebanon that have remained relatively stable.

Social Change: History and Conception

Masters of sociological thought had a special interest in, perhaps an obsession with, comprehending and predicting social change. The subject of social change loomed large in the writings of social scientists well before the birth of the discipline of sociology. It was the focus of attention of the medieval scholar, Ibn Khaldun, the father of Arab sociology, long before Comte, the founder of modern Western sociology, had written about it. Since then, students of society have been overwhelmed with works on social change by a variety of prominent sociologists, notably, Spencer, Durkheim, Tonnies, Marx, Weber, Parsons, and today's postmodern theorists.

Ibn Khaldun was eager to investigate the factors that cause prosperity of states, cities, and societies, and the ones that lead to their demise.[34] Auguste Comte contended that human societies pass through three consecutive stages: theological, then metaphysical, and finally positivistic. Like Comte, Herbert Spencer had his evolutionary theory but added that societies that evolve into more complex structures undergo differentiation in functions. Emile Durkheim's theory of division of labor and concepts of mechanic and organic solidarity also highlight his focus on social change. Durkheim was particularly worried about the adverse effects of social change on the traditional social bonds resulting in debilitated moral values and anomie. Karl Marx pointed to the power of history in replacing old, exploitative relations of production under capitalism with new, non-exploitative relations under socialism. Max Weber underscored the role of "rationalization" and the "Protestant ethic" in promoting economic progress in Europe. Tonnies distinguished between *Gemeinschaft* (community) features, which are characteristic of traditional societies, and *Gesellschaft* (society) features, which are characteristic of modern societies.

Parsons' theory of social action that embodies the "instrumental" and "expressive" types of action is another attempt at understanding the structural transition from traditional to modern society.[35] His theory is a testimony to the distinguished place of social change even among conservative functionalists.[36] Despite the great difference between the functionalist and conflict approaches, both have concentrated their efforts on studying social change. Functionalists view change as an expected measure in response to disturbance in stability while conflict theorists see it as a necessary step to the establishment of a new system. Functionalists describe change as an "adaptation" or "assimilation" to new circumstances while maintaining homeostasis whereas conflict theorists describe change as the negation of an archaic system and the emergence of a new, better alternative.

Postmodernist scholars show passionate involvement in the subject. Postmodernists like Anthony Giddens, Jurgen Haberman, Ulrich Beck, Pierre Bourdieu, Jean-Francois Lyotard, and Foucault have contributed each in his own way, to our understanding of the nature of Western societies in the 1990s. Although the focus of much of their work is the postmodern society in Europe and America, some of their ideas and themes may be relevant to the Lebanese case.[37]

The main reason for this relevance is the role the environment plays in social change. Lebanon cannot be an isolated entity in the contemporary world system that is characterized by interconnectedness, a system that has created new conditions for social change.[38]   Indeed, Lebanon is heavily influenced by major changes in the surrounding environment, such as socioeconomic and political transformations in the neighboring Arab and Middle Eastern countries.   Furthermore, the number of Lebanese emigrants exceeds that of residents, and a large segment of the emigrants, particularly in Europe and America, are in constant touch with their kin and friends in Lebanon. Such an interaction between emigrants and residents is bound to diffuse Western ideas and norms into Lebanon.

Another important reason for the likely relevance of postmodern themes and values is what Giddens calls "globalization of culture."[39] Themes related to modern and postmodern society have become part and parcel of a New World culture.[40] Such a process is bolstered by far-reaching changes in the world's political and economic orders and in the nature of technological advances.

In this study, social change refers to the various alterations in the social, economic, and political organization of society.   While other broader more encompassing definitions of social change include changes in the normative system, the one used in this book is fairly restricted. The rationale behind it is that the main thesis of the book hinges on the relation between social, political, and economic changes, on the one hand, and normative changes on the other.   This approach to the subject of social change may be termed "macrosociological."

"Macrosociology," or macro analysis, deals with general aspects of society, such as institutions and culture, while "microsociology," or microanalysis, focuses on daily personal encounters between people. The macro-micro division subsumes the old distinction between individual and society and the more recent agency-structure dualism. Some theorists suggest that there is a sociological macro-micro dualism that is similar to philosophical dualism, such as the separate and antagonistic entities good and evil.

Sociologists differ in the way they approach the macro-micro dualism. Parsons, for instance, was so obsessed with conformity and harmony that he neglected the creative "productive" dimension of social activity in favor of concentration on the stabilizing integrating dimension of social "reproduction."[41] By the same token, structural Marxists like Althusser were so keen on pinpointing the powerful effect of the economic institutions in capitalist society that the role of human beings was reduced to virtual insignificance.[42]

It is the view of this author that this dualism represents distinct, yet interconnected, aspects of society. Individual and society mutually affect each other but neither can attain full dominance over the other.[43] Man is neither totally free of social constraints and influences, nor a hapless victim of societal overarching forces. The former view is expressed by some symbolic interactionists and the latter by some functionalists and structural Marxists.[44]

The agent-structure dualism provides a more accurate description of the macro-micro dilemma. The term "agent" refers to a player who is active in creating changes in his/her social environment while being cognizant of social circumstances, ties, and constraints. An "agent" needs not be an individual; it can be a social group or collectivity, such as youth in this study. Some authors replace the term "agent" with "action" to highlight the active dimension of the concept. Unlike the individual, who may be perceived as a passive victim of the social world, the agent, according to Giddens, can make a difference in that world.[45]

However, while this study is in accordance with Giddens' view on the role of the agent, it does not follow with his view on the nature of the relationship between agent and structure. Giddens does not see any independent characteristics of social structures because he regards them as external to people. This study shares Layder's view that social systems are "partly independent of people's reasons and motivations."[46]

Employing this perspective, Lebanese youth are regarded as "agents" engaging in constant interaction with other relatively independent social institutions such as the family, school, and government agencies. Such a process involves negotiation and compromise, thereby, limiting the agent's ability to impose its will on the social institutions.

Culture, Structure, and Change

Sociologists have long debated the nature of the relationship between culture and social structure. According to Bourdieu and Alexander, culture is relatively independent from social structure.[47] Classical Marxists assert that "infrastructure," or the economic technological base of society, is the primary determinant of "superstructure," to which culture belongs. In stark opposition to Marxists, Max Weber contends that culture is the primary determinant of infrastructure.

Neither Marx nor Weber provides a satisfactory explanation for the nature of the relationship between culture and structure. It is the contention of this author that neither culture dominates structure nor the other way round; both interact with each other in a two-way process with the individual acting effectively to influence both. In other words, normative patterns and non-normative social systems are interdependent. Old norms influence social structure, and altered social structure can change old norms. It is also likely to find a "cultural lag" between innovations in technology and stagnation in normative patterns as historical evidence reveals.

The position incorporated in this study is in line with the insightful observation that Marx once made, and which Giddens supports. Marx noted that people "make their own history, but they do not make it just as they please; they do not make it under circumstances chosen by themselves, but under circumstances directly encountered, given and transmitted from the past."[48]

One way to describe these circumstances is through Bourdieu's notion of "habitus." "Habitus" refers to the knowledge—beliefs, norms and values—specific to particular cultures or subcultures that is acquired by people. Thus, one can speak of a middle-class way of dealing with authority figures as a middle-class "habitus" or of Muslims' attitudes toward women as a Muslim's "habitus". However, the notion of "habitus" is not carried to its extreme in this study by suggesting that people are passive victims who are totally under its sway. Instead, they are described as agents with power who can produce and reproduce social institutions and the circumstances in which they live.[49]

Another useful concept to employ in understanding the relation between culture and structure is Habermas's "lifeworld." It refers to the "way in which our activities and ideas are related to the institutional, economic, and cultural structure of the society in which we live."[50] By experiencing life in a particular community at a particular time, one acquires beliefs and values that shape attitudes and impact actions. The "lifeworld" brings together the effects of social norms, the role of personality traits, and that of the social system. It represents the concurrence of action and structure, which are relatively independent.[51] To avoid the macro-micro dualism, Habermas suggests a combined framework. For him, society is comprised of both a "sociocultural lifeworld" and a "social system."[52] Habermas, however, was ambiguous about the nature of the relation between system and the "lifeworld." In accordance with Layder, this study incorporates the view that system and "lifeworld" tend not to be separate, but interrelated aspects of society.[53]

Social reality is obviously very complex. It is composed of multiple systems, notably, economy, polity, and culture, which are linked together in a reciprocal causal manner.[54] In my opinion, these systems are interrelated in such a complicated manner that no single theory could capture them adequately. Therefore, a combination of theoretical perspectives that embrace a variety of concepts have been selected for this study. These concepts include Giddens' "agent" and "production and reproduction" of social life, Bourdieu's "habitus," and Habermas's "lifeworld." According to this approach, social behavior is strongly affected by norms and values in a society that is marked by inequality, power relations, and conflict.

A crucial step in the study approach is to place the value orientations and normative patterns of the Lebanese youth within their sociological and historical contexts.[55] In other words, the study takes into account both the changing and persistent characteristics of the Lebanese society that was subjected to various domestic and external influences. The most noted domestic influences are a long devastating civil war, a modified local demographic, and economic and political conditions. Significant external influences include a new regional political system and a new world order. These issues are tackled in depth in the next chapter.

Gender, Social Structure, and Values

"Gender" is a concept defined and maintained by society[56] while "sex"—being male or female—is a biological trait. "Gender" is "a central category for understanding oneself and others."[57] It is also the most organizing component of an individual's self-concept.[58] Social learning theory asserts that gender-related behavior among adults is rooted in early socialization; it is learned very early in life, between the ages of two and three.[59] Gender is sustained and reinforced by family, school, church, work settings and the media.[60] It is a social construction that determines many of the beliefs, expectations, roles, norms and values of men and women in a specific culture.

Gender stereotypes—in such domains as roles, occupations, and personality traits—are incorporated into our tacit or unconscious beliefs about people.[61] These beliefs consider men as rational, objective, decisive, aggressive, dominant, and independent and women as emotional, subjective, submissive, dependent, caring, and good at household chores and childrearing.[62] A man's success is often attributed to his ability, a woman's to luck.[63] In the West, despite the presence of egalitarian, conscious attitudes, gender-biased perceptions, probably unconscious, lead to discriminatory treatment.[64]

Gender is an integral part of the stratification system in society. In all contemporary societies, the distributions of rewards, prestige, and power are not equal between men and women. They are tilted in favor of men. In patriarchal societies, gender inequality, dominance of men, and subordination of women are enduring hallmarks. Hence, it is "difficult to separate gender, competence, leadership, power, and legitimacy."[65] Candidates for top positions in social institutions are assessed not only on ability but also, often implicitly, on the basis of their sex.

Eminent sociologists, like Durkheim and Parsons, justified gendered family structure in terms of necessary division of labor within the family. Parsons distinguished between "expressive" and "instrumental" tasks that separate "feminine" from "masculine" roles.[66] Building on such conservative, sexist views of women, some writers attribute women's assumption of subordinate roles to their passive and dependent nature. Recent research, however, shows that women tend to be passive and dependent as a result of occupying subordinate roles, not the other way round.[67]

In Arab societies, which are typical of patriarchal structures, gender is part and parcel of everyday life. Unlike the English language, the Arabic language is heavily gendered.   Adjectives, pronouns, and verbs can either be "feminine" or "masculine."   The distinction is as sharp as the segregation of the sexes in traditional Arab society. Nevertheless, languages can change and modernize, as can societies.

CHAPTER 3

RESEARCH REVIEW AND STUDY METHODOLOGY

> Typically, the scientific paper or monograph presents an immaculate appearance which reproduces little or nothing of the intuitive leaps, false starts, mistakes, loose ends, and happy accidents that actually cluttered up the inquiry. The public record of science therefore fails to provide many of the source materials needed to reconstruct the actual course of scientific developments.
>
> Robert Merton[1]

This chapter presents a brief review of relevant past research on norms of youth in various countries, with special reference to Lebanon. The review is suggestive rather than comprehensive. Its purpose is to highlight the different approaches and varied results of case studies. Subsequently, the methodology of the study is discussed, followed by a description of the background characteristics of the respondents.

Research Review

The literature abounds with studies either on social values and norms or on youth, particularly adolescents. Much less profuse are studies that deal with norms and values of college students, particularly during the past two decades. In the U.S., magazines such as *Time* and *Newsweek*, and several books by popular writers have repeatedly described the American youth of the 1980s and 1990s as self-centered, apathetic, and greedy.[2]   They argue that the so-called "X Generation" raised in postindustrial culture celebrates the self to the extent of immediate sensual gratification and eroticism.   Sociologist Daniel Bell warned that the youth's resentment of order and limits leads to nihilism.[3]

A major work that examines American youth is the national survey of freshman students conducted annually to monitor changes in their social norms.   Students entering college for the first time are questioned about a host of social and political issues.   Their responses are then compared with those of freshman students in earlier years.   Questions include the type and frequency of activities students were engaged in during the past year (religious, political, volunteering), amount of time spent studying in a typical week, political views, and importance of selected life goals (including raising a family, getting rich, becoming a community leader).   Pertinent to this study are the following findings, which conclude that American college Freshmen today:

- are more disengaged from politics
- show less participation in community action programs
- are middle-of-the-road politically
- place more importance on financial and personal success
- show a declining support for sexual freedom[4]

Several shorter studies on American youth have appeared in professional journals. These articles usually focus on few variables. For example, one article investigates time trends in social values of American youth, notably, personal self-fulfillment, political beliefs, and pursuit of material well being as a life goal.[5]   Another examines the relation of social environment to materialistic values.[6]   A third links social values with conformity and type of dress.[7]   A fourth reveals gender differences in the association of managerial style and personal values.[8]

In Western Europe, the European Value Systems Study Group conducted a major study of social values in 1981.[9]   This study expanded into the World Values Survey, a world project that reached non-European countries, particularly the U.S.A., Canada, and Australia.   A total of twenty-six countries were covered in sample surveys in 1990. Among its major findings are the following:

- Over 90% of the respondents consider the family to be very important in their lives.
- A minority of respondents has shown no tolerance toward some ethnic groups in their countries.
- Authority at the work place was less accepted in 1990 than in earlier years.
- There is a prevalence of post-materialist value orientations, such as the emphasis on self-expression and personal choice, as indicators of rising individualism and priority of quality of life issues over those of physical security.[10]

Further analysis of the World Values Survey resulted in a major work by Ronald Inglehart entitled, *Modernization and Postmodernization,* which examined economic, political, and cultural changes in forty-three societies. In the book, the author provides empirical evidence for a shift in social values of adults from traditionalism to modernity in some countries and from modernity to postmodernity in Europe and North America.[11]

In the Arab Middle East, research on norms and values that were published during the past three decades are classified into four broad categories. The first category includes general studies on the Arab world that integrated norms within other subjects such as the family, women, political systems, modes of living, and religion.[12] The second category of studies dealt with one particular country using an approach similar to that of the first category, that is, placing norms and values under other headings.[13] A third type is anthropological, focusing on specific communities such as tribes, villages, and city neighborhoods, within which norms were examined.[14] A fourth type dealt mainly with the subject of norms and values, some of which covered several Arab countries while others were restricted to one specific country.[15] To the aforementioned, one can add a variety of books and articles in the form of stories, autobiographies, and poems reflecting norms and values of various social groups in the Arab world.

Previous Research in Lebanon

In Lebanon, research on social norms and values either covered the entire society focusing on certain social groups and categories,[16] or examined specific small communities.[17] Furthermore, norms and values were often treated as part of other subjects. Since one of the objectives of this research is to investigate temporal changes in norms, it is useful to discuss comparable studies that examined attitudes or norms of students in pre-war Lebanon. To qualify as fully comparable, these studies should have used the same or very similar questions or variables, and covered the same survey population, i.e., Lebanese students at AUB and LU. Unfortunately, in the strict sense, no such study exists. What exists instead are several empirical studies of university students with which this study shares one to four variables or questions.

For example, there is Levon Melikian's study of the personality of Arab youth,[18] which is limited to a selected number of male Arab students at the AUB. In the study, Melikian employed a totally different instrument than the one employed here. He used an indirect technique of measurement, the projective technique, and particularly the "Thematic Apperception Test" that presents the subject with a set of ambiguous stimuli. Unlike Melikian's study of the structure of personality, the present study of attitudes and norms is able to get at the needed information by asking direct questions. Thus, there is no methodological justification for using an indirect technique. Furthermore, "because of the assumptions behind the inferences used in indirect methods, their validity is of special concern."[19] Still, it is useful to note the following relevant findings of Melikian:

- Arab male youth are more dependent on their parents than are their American counterparts, but are also more resentful of the parents' meddling in their affairs.[20]
- Arab male youth expect women to "accede to the demands" and whims of men. An assertive woman challenges the dominant role of man and threatens his perceived image of himself.[21]
- According to Arab male youth, sex outside marriage is condoned for men but is deemed indecent for women.[22]

A more related work, by Levon Melikian and Lutfy Diab, focuses on group affiliations of AUB students.[23] One problem with using this source as baseline data on AUB students relates to the nature of its survey population, which consists of both Lebanese and non-Lebanese Arab students. However, this comparison is reasonable if we restrict it to social and family norms and assume that the social structure in Arab societies in the early 1970s had several common elements, notably, the dominant role of the family. Another methodological problem arises when Melikian and Diab's data are used, namely, that their sample is a non-probability sample while the one used in this book is a probability sample. This poses as a problem as findings from non-probability samples are not generalizable to the total population.

A third methodological difference between Melikian and Diab's study and the present one is the different indicators used to measure group affiliations. Melikian and Diab used a forty-two item, forced choice questionnaire, while in this study, questions on group affiliation were of the rank-order type.[24] Furthermore, the forced choice approach is less effective because it creates for the respondent a hypothetical, unrealistic situation, whereas in real life, he/she has a number of alternative choices, which the rank-order question provides. However, the findings of Melikian and Diab are quite plausible and consistent with those of the present study, as elaborated in chapter 5, despite the different methodological approaches. Therefore, Melikian and Diab's data are used as baseline data in chapter 5.

A third partially comparable study is Theodor Hanf's survey of political attitudes of Lebanese university students in 1971.[25] Only one question on political orientation is comparable, while two other questions on preferred political leaders are partially comparable since they were combined into one in the survey used in this study. Still, Hanf's relevant findings will be presented in chapter 7.

Nathat Nasr and Monte Palmer[26] dealt with the relation between alienation and political attitudes among university students, which this study does not examine closely. It also used broad, general items to measure the "general regard" for political institutions, including the desire for change, while this study uses more specific items and open-ended questions. Again, despite the limited comparability of their data and the data of this study, their relevant findings are presented in chapter 7.

Of all the related studies in the pre-war period, Halim Barakat's[27] is most comparable to the present study. In his study of political and social attitudes, Barakat focused on students' political orientations and the students' movement in the 1970s. His basic thesis was that vertical loyalties (such as religion and kinship) are more significant than horizontal loyalties (social class) "in determining student political radicalism and alienation in Lebanon."[28]   By contrast, this study is not restricted to student politics.   It covers a broader ground: students' individual values, their perceptions of societal values, and their political and family norms.   Barakat's sample covered three major universities whereas the sample used in this study covered two.   However, of all the studies completed in the pre-war period, Barakat's has the most common items with this study, even though the similarities are few.   A detailed comparison between the two studies is provided in chapters 6 and 7.

In terms of the political component of the research instrument, the most comparable study is by Hilal Khashan.[29]   In fact, several questions on political attitudes and values were deliberately extracted from his work[30] in order to make the findings of the two studies comparable.   However, its data were collected during the war period in 1988 when Lebanon, as Khashan rightly cautioned his readers, was experiencing "intense political uncertainty."[31]   Not only would this situation influence students' responses, but it would also make it almost impossible to design and implement a probability sample survey.   Furthermore, since they do not refer to the pre-war period, his data cannot serve as a baseline for comparing pre-war with postwar attitudes.   Another difficulty in comparing Khashan's data set with the data generated in this study is that his findings, which refer to six universities, are not broken down by university (except those pertaining to religiosity), whereas the data from this study refer to two universities.   Still, the relevant findings of Khashan's study are presented for comparison in chapter 7.

Since the end of hostilities in 1990, there seems to have been only one systematic scientific study, by al-Amin and Faour,[32] of the social values and norms of a substantial social group or category such as students, women, or workers.   All the other studies are either essays written by impassioned concerned scholars drawing on their personal observations and experience,[33] or analytical essays interlaced with data from non-representative samples.[34]   While these studies can provide useful insight into the research problem, their data limitations and subjectivity do not allow any generalization of their findings to the entire social group or society they investigated.

The study by al-Amin and Faour is a survey conducted in 1997 (hereafter referred to as the 1997 survey) that covered students in all institutions of higher learning in Lebanon using clustered sampling.   The 1997 questionnaire has three items that have close counterparts in the

1995 and 1996 questionnaires of this study, namely, a question on the most preferred politician, another on the most hated politician, and a third on the frequency of practicing religious rites. There are also a few common items between the 1997 questionnaire and each of 1993 and 1994 questionnaires of this study, namely, the questions on preferred religion of mate, religion of best friend, and attitude toward secularism and civil marriage. Although these items were not measured using exactly the same questions, it is instructive to compare the findings. Relevant results of the 1997 survey will be compared with results of this study in chapters 5 through 7.

Methodology

Unlike comparable preceding studies that were based on data collected in a single survey, this study is based on four recent surveys of Lebanese students aged 17-24 years. These surveys include a stratified random sample of AUB students in 1993; two quota-samples of AUB students in 1994 and 1996; and a purposive sample of LU students in 1996.

The 1993 AUB sample was a probability sample of the stratified random type. It was drawn from a list of students supplied by the Registrar's office at AUB and stratified by major. Like other probability samples, the distribution of this sample by the usual background variables is generalized to all students. The margin of error was below 3%, the response rate was 96%, and the sample size was 795 students.

The surveys conducted in the spring of 1994 and the spring of 1996 were quota samples based on the 1993 distribution of students by major. Such a distribution tends to be stable over a period of a few years, and conducting a quota-sample survey is less costly and easier to administer than a probability sample survey. Despite the non-probability nature of quota samples, their data tend to be reliable if the quotas are based on data from a recent census or probability sample survey. A 1991 quota-sample survey of AUB students conducted by this author has several common questions with the 1993 probability sample survey. The findings from these two surveys were highly consistent with no statistically significant differences.

Interviewers in the 1994 and 1996 surveys, who were students taking the research methods course in sociology, were assigned specified faculties. For example, one interviewer selected and interviewed a sample of medical students, another a sample of engineering students.   Each interviewer was in charge of selecting approximately twenty respondents from a particular major; these respondents had to include both male and female students who belonged to various religious sects and came from different provinces (*muhafazat*). The response rates in the 1994 and 1996 samples were very high: 96% and 97%, respectively. The numbers of students interviewed in 1994 and 1996 were 444 and 641, respectively.

As for LU students, a stratified random sample could not be drawn partly because a complete, recent list of students—i.e., a sampling frame—was not available. More importantly, at LU, access to a simple random sample of students is extremely difficult, for many students neither attend classes on a regular basis, nor are they physically present on campus most of the time. Halim Barakat faced the same problem in his survey of LU students in the early 1970s, which he tackled by employing mass-administered questionnaires in classrooms. This study resorted to the same method in November and December of 1996.

The LU survey population included all the faculties in Greater Beirut (branches I and II) in order to ensure adequate representation of various majors, religious sects, and provinces. At each of the faculties, all students attending a selected number of classes completed the questionnaire in the presence of Professor Najwa Yahfoufi, a social psychologist at the Lebanese University. It was operationally more efficient to limit the selection to those classes that had twenty or more students. Typically, class size ranged between twenty-five and thirty-five students. The use of a mass-administered questionnaire and the presence of a LU faculty member to ascertain the importance of the students' opinions to the researchers and of the confidentiality of responses resulted in the exceptionally high response rate of 99%. The number of completed questionnaires was 1013.

The Data

The data set includes a host of social values and norms including the following:

- Individual values such as equalitarianism, individualism, authoritarianism, and fatalism.
- Societal values relating to manual work, team work, face saving,

and tribal solidarity.

- Values and norms concerning family issues such as respect for parents, priority of the family to the individual over other group affiliations, and close ties with kin.

- Attitudes and norms concerning gender issues such as the modesty code for women, the traditional role of women as wives and mothers, and gender stereotypes. Among the widely known stereotypes is the belief that women are inferior to men and are emotional not rational. Other stereotypes call for women to stay home; in case of financial need, traditional norms approve of their work outside the home but only in "feminine" jobs.

- Attitudes and norms concerning political issues such as sectarianism, parochial loyalties, and acceptance to coexist with members of other religious sects.

- As elaborated in chapters 5-7, most of the questions in the survey questionnaires were drawn from other studies that had subjected them to tests of validity and reliability.   Still, all three questionnaires were first tested for face validity by asking over twenty students and a couple of colleagues to comment on the clarity of each question and on whether or not it measures a specified variable or concept.   The questionnaires were then pre-tested with a sample of thirty students, after which minor editorial changes were introduced.

Indices in the processed data were validated both internally and externally.   Internal validation refers to the item analysis of the components of each index whereby the independent contribution of each item to the composite index is assessed.   If the contribution of a given item is negligible, it should be excluded from the index.   External validation refers to the relationships between the index and external indicators of the given variable, i.e., indicators that are not part of the index.[35]   This is based on expected relationships among variables.   For example, external validation for the index of religiosity was verified by testing whether highly religious people are more attached to their religious groups than non-religious people.   A second way of verification is to find members of the lower class politically more radical than members of the upper class.

The quality of data was also verified with two tests of reliability.

First, a number of internal consistency checks were made between various combinations of variables. For example, in the 1996 questionnaire, the frequency of practicing religious rituals was cross-tabulated with the question on religious affiliation and with the question on degree of importance of religion to the respondent. In all of the questionnaires, the questions on father's education and occupation were cross-tabulated.

The second test of reliability was that of equivalence reliability for multiple indicators of constructs. Cochran chi-square was computed as part of the analysis of variance testing for reliability of the items that comprise each of the indices used in the study. The indices used are unidimensional in the sense that each taps one dimension of the variable in question. Unidimensionality was ascertained first conceptually by requesting the judgement of a selected number of students and colleagues as to whether or not the indicators that compose each index measure one dimension of the given variable. Statistical verification of unidimensionality usually resorts to factor analysis, which requires intervally-scaled items. Since the items in the constructed indices are dichotomous, analysis of variance was used instead. It must also be remarked that the consistency in the results of the 1991 and 1993 surveys provided strong evidence for the reliability of the core of the 1991 questionnaire that was re-tested in 1993.

The Respondents

The numbers of men and women in all the data samples are large enough to allow separate statistical analyses by sex. At AUB, there is almost a sex balance among students, with more females than males in the 1995-96 sample. At LU, the majority of respondents (62%) are females (table 3.1) due to the dominance of females in humanities and social sciences which represent the majors of half the interviewees (table 3.2). Still, all the fields of specialization that are offered at the two selected universities are included. In both universities, the largest faculty is that of arts and sciences, with higher student enrollment in arts than in sciences (table 3.2). This uneven distribution of students by major is most pronounced at LU.

Another important reason for the uneven distribution by major is that large proportions of poor and lower middle-class students, who form the majority of the student body at LU, choose the arts major. Their choice is dictated by financial reasons. They cannot devote all their time to studying; they need to earn their living by taking at least a part-time job. Therefore, since only humanities and social sciences departments can accommodate part-timers, these students join them.

The respondents come from different social class backgrounds. One indicator of social class is the father's occupation. As expected, there is a significant difference between AUB and LU with regard to the occupational composition of students' fathers. About one-third of AUB students have fathers with professional and highly technical occupations, as compared with only 9% of their LU counterparts (table 3.3). Owners and managers of big business enterprises are fathers to about a quarter of AUB students, but only to 8% of LU students. Most LU students have fathers who are employed either as white-collar workers (38%) or blue-collar workers (26%).

Table 3.1: Percentage Distribution of Students by Sex, University, and Year

| | AUB (%) | | | LU (%) |
Sex	1992/93	1993/94	1995/96	1995/96
Male	57	56	47	38
Female	43	44	53	62
Number of Students	795	444	641	1003

Table 3.2: Percentage Distribution of Students by Major, University, and Year

| | AUB (%) | | | LU (%) |
Major	1992/93	1993/94	1995/96	1996/97
Engineering & Agriculture	31	32	22	5
Medicine & Health Sciences	12	17	12	8
Sciences	23	18	22	36
Humanities & Social Sciences	34	33	44	51
Number of Students	795	444	641	1003

Table 3.3: Percentage Distribution of Students by Father's Occupation
University, and Year*

Father's Occupation	AUB(%)			LU (%)
	1992/93	1993/94	1995/96	1996/97
Professional & Technical	27	30	32	9
Owner/Manager of Big Business	24	23	22	8
Small Business & Self-employed	17	21	23	19
White-collar Salaried Worker	24	17	19	38
Skilled & Unskilled Worker	8	9	4	26
Number of Students	**745**	**376**	**586**	**802**

* Missing, retired, and disabled cases were excluded.

Table 3.4: Percentage Distribution of Students by Social Class*, University, and
Year

Social Class	AUB (%)			LU (%)
	1992/93	1993/94	1995/96	1996/97
Upper	51	53	54	17
Middle	41	38	42	57
Lower	8	9	4	26
Number of Students	**745**	**376**	**586**	**802**

* Upper class refers to students whose fathers are professionals, business owners or managers, middle class to fathers who are self-employed or white-collar employees, lower class to skilled and unskilled workers.

Using the father's occupation as a proxy for social class identification, the respondents were classified into three classes: upper, middle, and lower. Children of professionals, high-ranking officers in public agencies and the armed forces, owners and managers of big business establishments (for example, banks, supermarkets, schools, and factories) were considered part of the upper class. Children of small-business owners (including small retail shops, grocery stores, bookshops,

Table 3.5: Percentage Distribution of Students by Father's Education,
University, and Year

| Father's Education | AUB (%) | | | LU (%) |
	1992/93	1993/94	1995/96	1996/97
Illiterate	0	0	0	4
Completed Primary	6	10	2	21
Completed Intermediate	10	6	7	27
Completed Secondary	27	31	23	24
Completed University	57	53	68	24
Number of Students	**795**	**410**	**641**	**1003**

pharmacies), self-employed businessmen, and salaried white-collar workers belong to the middle class. The lower-class tag was assigned to those whose fathers are skilled and unskilled wage earners. According to this classification, the majority of AUB students have an upper-class background while the majority of LU students belong to the middle-class, and a substantial proportion (26%) to the lower class (table 3.4).

In addition to father's occupation, three other indicators of social background include the father's education, the mother's education, and the mother's occupation. Again, the data show clear differences between AUB and LU students. The majority of AUB students have fathers with college degrees, as compared to a quarter of LU students (table 3.5). Another quarter of LU students have fathers with a primary education or less. In other words, the fathers are functionally illiterate; primary education does not provide adequate comprehension of the complex phenomena in today's world, a requirement for survival in a highly competitive society like Lebanon.

A higher percentage of LU students (29%) have mothers with a primary education or less. Of those, a third are illiterate. By contrast, none of the mothers of AUB students are illiterate, and close to half (44%) have college degrees (table 3.6). At LU, only 12 % of the mothers have completed a university education.

In 1996, most mothers of students at both AUB and LU were out of the job market, playing their traditional role as mothers and housewives: 79% at LU versus 57% at AUB (table 3.7). Nevertheless, there were more professionals among the working mothers of AUB

Table 3.6: Percentage Distribution of Students by Mother's Education
University, and Year

Mother's Education	AUB (%)			LU (%)
	1992/93	1993/94	1995/96	1996/97
Illiterate	1	2	0	10
Completed Primary	6	9	4	19
Completed Intermediate	12	11	9	31
Completed Secondary	48	49	43	28
Completed University	33	29	44	12
Number of Students	**795**	**442**	**641**	**1003**

Table 3.7: Percentage Distribution of Students by Mother's Occupation
University, and Year*

Mother's Occupation	AUB (%)			LU (%)
	1992/93	1993/94	1995/96	1996/97
Professional & technical	3	5	10	2
Owners/managers of big business	4	3	5	1
Small business & self-employed	2	3	3	1
White-collar salaried worker	23	16	23	14
Skilled & unskilled worker	1	1	2	3
Homemaker	67	72	57	79
Number of Students	**790**	**444**	**629**	**1013**

* Missing, retired, and disabled cases were excluded

students than of LU students (10% versus 2%). Moreover, it should be noted that the majority of working mothers of AUB students were white-collar employees.

Since religious sect is a central social group with which people identify, students were asked to report their sects. All the six major religious sects—Maronite, Catholic, and Orthodox Christians, Sunni and Shiite Muslims, and the Druze—are represented in the samples with numbers adequate for statistical analysis. The majority of students at

Table 3.8: Percentage Distribution of Students by Religious Sect, University, and Year

| Religious sect | AUB (%) | | | LU (%) |
	1992/93	1993/94	1995/96	1996/97
Maronite	13	14	12	29
Catholic	6	7	8	7
Orthodox	15	17	15	8
Sunni	35	33	31	15
Shiite	19	18	18	30
Druze	9	9	12	8
Other & Missing	3	2	4	3
Number of Students	**795**	**444**	**641**	**1003**

Table 3.9: Percentage Distribution of Students by Parents' Place of Residence, University, and Year

| Parents' Residence | AUB (%) | | | LU (%) |
	1992/93	1993/94	1995/96	1996/97
Outside Lebanon	5	6	15	0
Beirut & Suburbs	62	68	50	52
Other areas of Mount Lebanon	10	9	12	27
Southern Lebanon	7	6	8	10
Northern Lebanon	12	9	9	6
Beqa'	4	2	6	5
Number of Students	**795**	**441**	**641**	**1003**

both universities are Muslims (table 3.8).   At AUB, Sunnis, as a sect, comprise the largest group of respondents (31% in 1995/96).   At LU, Shiite Muslims and Maronite Christians form the two largest religious groups in the sample (about 30% each).   This sectarian, bimodal distribution reflects the predominance of Shiite students on the LU campuses of West Beirut and its suburbs and the predominance of Maronite students on the LU campuses of East Beirut and its suburbs. In the former area, the large majority of the population is Muslim; in the latter, the population is overwhelmingly Christian.

By comparison, in 1972-73, Sunnis, as a sect, also comprised the largest group of students (33%). However, Christian students from the various sects combined were the majority: 57%.[36] At LU, Halim Barakat's sample in 1970 included a majority of Christians at 54 %, most of whom were Maronites.[37]

Parochial ties continue to mark Lebanese society. Therefore, it was important that the sample covered various districts of the country. The data indicate that students at LU and at AUB come from all the regions of Lebanon: the capital, Mount Lebanon, North, South, and the Beqa'. At AUB, 15% of the parents are living abroad, mainly in the Arab Gulf countries where many Lebanese emigrated during the war seeking employment. At least half the parents live in the capital and its fringes. At LU, over a quarter of the parents live in the Metn and Kesrwan regions of Mount Lebanon, the long-time heartland of the Maronites, as compared to 12% of their AUB counterparts (table 3.9). Only a minority of students have parents residing in each of the three other districts or *muhafazat*.

CHAPTER 4

STABILITY AND CHANGE IN SOCIAL STRUCTURE

> If the government's authoritarian attitudes are shared
> by civil society, democrats may well view the latter as
> part of the problem rather than part of the solution.
>
> Iliya Harik[1]

Which aspects of Lebanon's social structure, if any, have changed and which have persisted over the past three decades? This is the central question addressed here since the nature of changes in social structure is thought to influence the normative pattern. In all certainty, not all changes in social structure directly impinge on norms and values. For that reason, only those changes that can affect norms in a known or hypothesized manner will be presented. Subsumed under social structure are demography, economy, political system, religion, education, and family. Since the elements of the social structure are subject to a variety of external influences, examination of these influences is in order.

Demography

The forces of social change and civil war in Lebanon have joined hands in influencing virtually all factors of demographic change: mortality, fertility, and population movement. The primary cause of mortality change is the acts of violence that pervaded Lebanon through fifteen years of war. The fierce battles between domestic factions and military incursions by Israel, notably, the 1982 invasion, along with its air raids and bombardment of villages killed and maimed tens of thousands of residents. The exact war toll is not known and estimates vary widely by source. The most qualified source is the Lebanese "internal security force" or police, whose most recent estimates were lower than earlier ones, putting the death toll at well under 100,000 persons.

War-related deaths among Lebanese citizens had a direct effect on the total population, particularly young adults, 15-29 years of age. The size of the total population diminished, and the age structure was altered due to the loss of the young who were the core force of combatants. The high death rate among the young is reflected in the proportion of widowed women aged 40-49 in 1994-96 (6%).[2] These women were 20-29 years old in 1975, the prime age for marriage. Since husbands tend to be five years older on average than their wives, the husbands of those women are expected to have been 25-34 years old in 1975. This cohort of men was most affected by war-related mortality.

In addition to war-inflicted deaths, emigration is another factor that had the same effect on the total population and the age structure. As the intensity of violence continued to escalate and the war seemed to fester indefinitely, the people kept paying a heavier toll every day on their lives, personal property, jobs, and psychological well being. Eventually, many heads of families and young members had no option but to emigrate. They were encouraged by family and friends to seek a better life abroad. The majority of emigrants were young and middle-aged adults who left for either the Arab Gulf states or North America and Australia. Again, their accurate number is not known, and available estimates vary widely by source from a few hundred thousand to over a million. Nevertheless, the consequences of international migration for the age structure of the population can be examined quantitatively through analysis of the 1996 housing and population survey.

In 1970, the number of the Lebanese aged 10-24 was about 645,000. This age cohort was 15-29 years old in 1975 when the civil war broke out. In 1994-96, or 1995 as an approximation, this cohort was 35-49 years old. Its number was about 540,000 persons, a drop of 105,000.[3] Death by natural causes and accidents among this age category is not the primary cause of this decline, for it can only account for a very small percentage of deaths. The two major causes of the decline are war-related deaths and out-migration. It is almost impossible to separate out these two effects due to the lack of required data. Nonetheless, the conclusion is unequivocal: there is a considerable alteration in the age structure of the population (compare figures 4.1 and 4.2).

Social change and civil strife also affected the population movement, which comprises internal and international migration. Internal migration attained more importance than it ever had among demographic variables. The flux of people among various regions for many years has destabilized the geographic distribution of the population. Besides tens of thousands of urban-bound people seeking employment, some 800,000 people were forcefully displaced from their original domiciles during the years of 1975-1990. Many have returned to their homes or villages since the fighting has stopped. Others, who have not returned, established satisfactory lives for themselves in other places of Lebanon, thereby, deterring them from returning. Some of the displaced refused to return because of the lack of public services in their native villages, or the shortage of funds to rebuild their demolished houses and businesses. In addition, the memories of past horrors overshadowed the government's assurances that the war was over. The wounds of these displaced people have not yet healed.

Duration of residence in each of the districts provides a good idea about the scale of geographic mobility. Table 4.1 shows that most of the residents in each and every *muhafaza* have moved to their current *muhafaza* of residence during the war period. A significant percentage of current residents are recent, internal migrants. Between 17 and 26 % of the population in each of the *muhafazat* have moved to their current residences after the war ended in 1990. Short-term residence results in building temporary social relations with new neighbors for a few years. This is likely to influence students' behavior and norms in ways that are contingent on the nature of those relations. If the new neighbors belong to the same family, social class, and religion, one's beliefs and norms are likely to be reinforced and social behavior stabilized. However, if the new neighbors are perceived as alien to the culture or belong to social groups with which the student does not identify, then a state of rejection, withdrawal, or dispute may arise between the old and the new residents.

This type of short-term residence yielded a diversity of outcomes that were observed in Lebanon during the past two decades. For example, Christians who were displaced from the Chouf to East Beirut, its fringes, and other towns were first received as friendly co-religionists. As time went by, old residents abhorred the presence of the newcomers in their communities. Not only did they dislike the lifestyle of the new migrants but they also perceived them as a threat to the prevailing, local

Figure 4.1: Adjusted Age-Sex Distribution of the Population of Lebanon, 1970

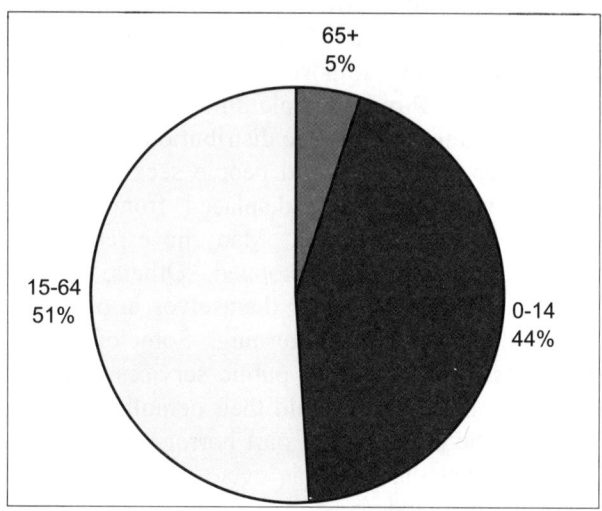

Figure 4.2: Adjusted Age-Sex Distribution of the Population of Lebanon, 1996

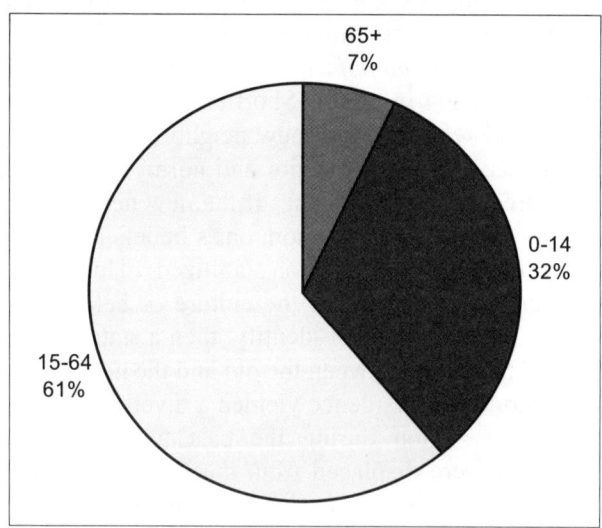

Table 4.1: Percentage of Distribution of the Population of Lebanon by Current
Place of Residence and Duration of Residence, 1996

Current Residence	Duration of Residence in Years				
	Over 21 (before 1974)	7-21	Less than 7	Total	Number of Cases
Beirut	48	35	17	100	380,418
Mount Lebanon	33	41	26	100	1,110,926
North Lebanon	40	39	21	100	651,022
South Lebanon	38	40	22	100	462,785
Beqa'	44	39	17	100	388,152

power structure. For instance, in the town of Jounieh, north of Beirut, a recent in-migrant was usually described as a "stranger" (*ghreeb*). By the same token, Sunni Muslims who fled Beirut for the largely Sunni city of Saida in the South were not always treated like members of the indigenous population. For example, many shopkeepers overcharged them for the goods they purchased. Also, Shiite Muslims who fled war-ravaged areas to safer places in West Beirut or Saida, where the majority are Sunni Muslims, were perceived to pose a threat to the homogeneity and power structure of local communities. The in-migrants were different from the longtime residents in more ways than one: they had a rural origin, belonged to a lower social class, and held "unorthodox" religious beliefs.

The recurrent flow of sizeable migration streams within the country since the onset of the war generated a new geographic distribution of the population. Between 1970 and 1996, Beirut's share of the total population dropped appreciably from 22 to 13 % (figures 4.3 and 4.4). By contrast, the proportion of residents of the *muhafazat* of North Lebanon, South Lebanon, and Beqa' jumped from 17, 12, and 10 % respectively to 21, 16, and 13 %. Little change has occurred to the proportion living in Mount Lebanon: a slight drop from 39 to 37 %. Beirut city proper lost population in both absolute and relative numbers due to a host of factors, namely, destruction of the city center where many residents lived, outward movement of former residents beyond its frontiers, and the tendency of newly wed Beirutis to live in the suburbs for economic reasons. As a result, the suburbs grew at the expense of

Beirut such that the *muhafaza* of Beirut (Beirut city proper) is no longer a meaningful administrative and economic unit. Instead, Greater Beirut, the metropolitan area that includes a good part of Mount Lebanon housing over 40% of the total population, is now the hub of economic and political activities in Lebanon.

This rise in the proportion of residents in the regions outside Greater Beirut calls for the government's attention to plan development projects in those areas. In addition to their larger demographic size, those areas continue to lag behind the capital in a number of important socio-demographic variables. While Lebanon as a whole has made significant strides in socio-economic development despite the protracted war, rural areas are still deficient in public services and score low on development indicators. The most underprivileged are the rural, remote villages of Akkar in North Lebanon, as evident in the various indicators of social development such as literacy rate, female mean age at first marriage, and income per capita.

The third demographic factor that the forces of social change and war have left their marks on is human fertility. The indicators of human fertility, both current and cumulative, have declined appreciably since 1971. The ratio of children 0-4 years to women 15-49 years (known as child-woman ratio) has dropped from 763 in 1971, to 313 children per 1000 women in 1996. The number of children ever born to women aged 45-49 (the oldest age group in which women are fecund) was 4.2 births per woman in 1996, down from 5.2 births per woman in 1971; this rate measures cumulative fertility or completed family size. Total fertility rate, which measures current fertility, has also dropped considerably from 4.6 in 1971, to 2.8 births per woman in 1996.[4]

Fertility measures show telling variations among the different *muhafazat*. On all measures, North Lebanon has the highest fertility rates while Beirut city and Mount Lebanon have the lowest rates; South Lebanon and Beqa' occupy a middle position. For example, the average number of children ever born to ever-married women is 2.8 per woman in Beirut but 4.2 in North Lebanon. The total fertility rate is 1.7 births per woman in Beirut, but twice that figure in North Lebanon: 3.4 births per woman (table 4.2). As to the current use of contraceptive methods, it is least prevalent in the north. It can then be inferred that the locus of poverty and underdevelopment has shifted from the *muhafaza* of South Lebanon, which was least developed before 1975, to the postwar North, particularly the populous district of Akkar. Still, rural areas of the South

Figure 4.3: Geographic Distribution of the Population of Lebanon, 1970

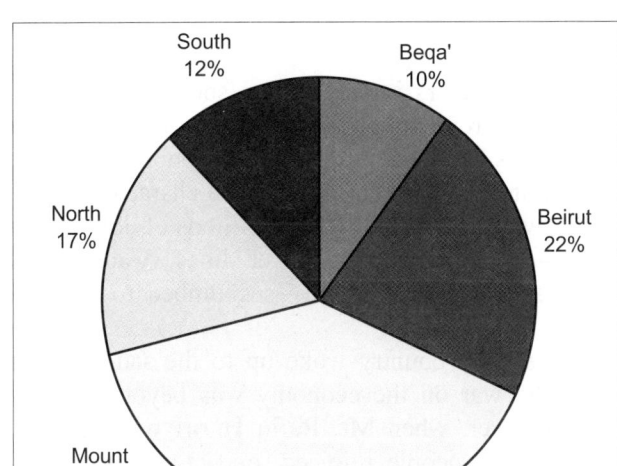

Figure 4.4: Geographic Distribution of the Population of Lebanon, 1996

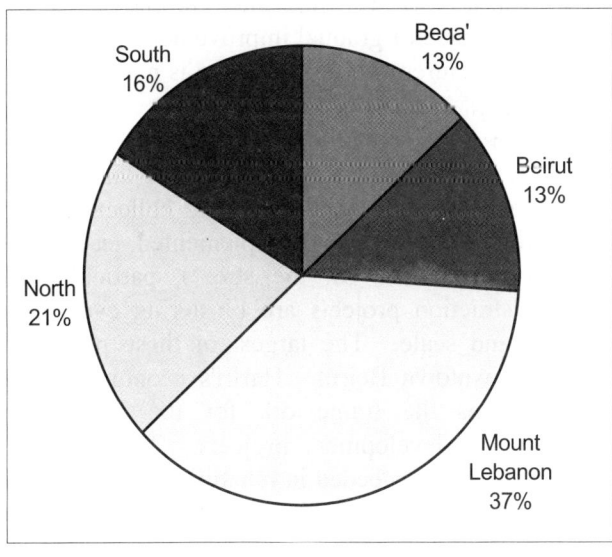

and Beqa' remain less developed than the capital and Mount Lebanon.

The Economy

A host of economic factors impinge upon society's values and norms: economic growth, productivity, inflation, employment, and income. After many years of strife, Lebanon's economy crumbled miserably, yet maintained its free-market, laissez-faire character. Losses in property, public and private alike, amounted to billions of dollars. The country's infrastructure—including roads, power lines, water supply system, and the solid waste disposal system—succumbed to the cruel forces of destruction.

Once peace reigned, the country woke up to the sad economic reality. The impact of the war on the economy was beyond anyone's wildest imagination. However, when Mr. Rafiq Hariri was appointed Prime Minister in 1993, most people rejoiced, expecting his business success worldwide to salvage Lebanon's economy. This newfound confidence in the country's future encouraged capitalists to invest. Between 1993 and 1996, the economy grew at an impressive pace, mainly through private investment. By implementing tight monetary policies, the government succeeded in ending the erratic fluctuation in the exchange rate of the Lebanese currency in relation to the U.S. dollar and other international currencies. As a result, the currency was first stabilized, then underwent a course of gradual improvement. In spite of the government's economic measures, the inflation rate is not quite under control. It reached an estimated 15 % in 1995.[5]

For the first time in many years, the Ministry of Finance has regained most of the power it lost during the war. Income taxes, power and utility bills, and indirect taxes on many items are collected. New finance laws and procedures were enacted and implemented, leading to a substantial rise in public revenues. On the streets, particularly in metropolitan Beirut, reconstruction projects are blustering everywhere with unprecedented vigor and scale. The largest of these projects is currently taking place in downtown Beirut. Hariri's economic master plan, Horizon 2000, provides the framework for the current and prospective reconstruction and development projects. Though overly ambitious, Hariri's plan has so far succeeded in rehabilitating a good part of the country's infrastructure. A considerable amount of work has been

Table 4.2: Selected Indicators of Fertility and Family Planning in Lebanon by Muhafaza, 1996

Muhafaza	Average Number of Children Ever Born Per Ever-Married Woman	Total Fertility Rate (Births During Last 3 Years Per Woman)	%Currently Married Women Using Any Method of Birth Control	Number of Women
Beirut	2.8	1.7	62.3	383
Mount Lebanon	3.0	2.0	64.4	1053
North Lebanon	4.2	3.4	53.2	613
South Lebanon	3.5	2.7	57.7	261
Nabatiyeh	3.6	2.6	58.6	159
Beqa'	3.9	2.5	66.4	366

Source of material: Maternal and Child Health Survey of Lebanon, 1996, Ministry of Social Affairs, Lebanon

completed in repairing and upgrading electric power, water and solid waste management systems, and the telephone and communication system. New bridges, roads, and highways were built, and others are under way.

As life returned to normal in postwar Lebanon, a steep demand arose for consumer durable goods. Soon the country's trade deficit hiked to an all-time high level of 50% of the Gross Domestic Product in 1994. As for the budget deficit, it has been high since 1993, exceeding 40% of expenditures in 1995 and it is expected to be at about that level in 1998. In 1996, the national debt accounted for about 40% of budgetary spending.[6]

Economic growth in postwar Lebanon did little to narrow the gap between the rich and the poor. On the contrary, there is evidence of a growing rift between the "have's" and the "have-not's." While no reliable detailed statistics on this subject exist, a cursory look at the results of the "1997 Study of Living Conditions of Households"[7] in Lebanon is very disconcerting. About 60% of households in Lebanon earn under $800 per month and 20% earn under $325, a bleak account knowing that the average household size is close to five persons. It is not a sign of economic health when the minimum legal wage ($250 per month) is below the line of extreme poverty. A family of five is considered extremely poor when its total earnings are below $300 per month. Careful observers who have past knowledge of Lebanon can recognize a new pattern of social polarization. Contributing to this skewed, pyramidal, class structure are a number of factors:

- War-related factors such as the impoverishment of a large segment of the population due to loss of jobs, property, displacement, or physical impairment.

- A combination of moderate inflation rate, rising indirect taxes, and low income tax for the upper-income brackets. This combination has lowered the purchasing power, thus the standard of living of the salaried workers estimated at 65% of the work force.[8] By contrast, capitalists have been amassing more fortunes by enjoying lower taxes (assuming that they accurately report their earnings). Rather than tax the wealthy that have the means to contribute to the public revenue, the government is targeting the middle and lower classes. Hariri's economic policy, much like former President Reagan's in the U.S.A., assumed that the poor will benefit from a trickle-down effect of economic growth, a growth that requires huge capital. To lure such capital into investing in Lebanon, the government decided to offer it highly favorable tax and work conditions. The paradox is that such conditions cannot be favorable to Lebanese workers in the short term, even if they are favorable in the long term. The short-term importance cannot be summarily dismissed because the poor cannot wait years down the line to eat. Food, health, and shelter are basic immediate needs for all people.

- The inefficiency and continuous corruption in many public agencies, which result in loss of substantial revenues for the government. Unwilling to break their wartime habits, thousands of households do not pay their utility bills. In response, the government is planning new ways of collecting public dues. As for corruption, it prevails unabashed in many public agencies. The scandalous story of Ra'fat Sulayman, the public officer who disappeared with millions of dollars stolen from the finance ministry and was then found dead and mutilated, is a poignant, sad illustration.

The Political System

Thirty years ago, Michael Hudson faced great difficulty in classifying Lebanon's political system in terms of known typologies because of its incoherent components:

> Lebanon is a democracy, but it is also an oligarchy....It is stable enough to attract enormous amounts of capital, yet a radio speech or a thrown rock can send the country into turmoil. Reform movements are as routine as corruption. Cabinet crises are chronic. The party system is feeble, yet public opinion is politically volatile.[9]

Today, despite the immense changes in various aspects of the political system, some of the above contradictions continue to exist, albeit in a different form. Whether or not Lebanon is a democracy depends on how one defines "democracy." This notion is so appealing to Arabs that no Arab regime has declared itself undemocratic. To be sure, "democracy" means different things to different people. Yet, there is some consensus among scholars that existing "democratic" nations share a set of features that comprise the minimum requirements for political democracy. These requirements, as formulated by the noted political scientist Robert Dahl, are:

- The constitution should give elected officials the right to control government policy decisions.
- Elections are held regularly under no or limited government coercion. The elections should be both free and fair.
- All adult citizens (except the mentally incapacitated and the senile) have a constitutional right to vote.
- All sane, law-abiding, adult citizens can run for public office.
- Freedom of expression is a constitutional right for citizens that is safeguarded by leaders and elected officials. Using that right poses no risk to the individual's personal freedom or security.
- Non-governmental sources of information, including those that oppose the government, are accessible to citizens.
- Citizens have the legal right to form political parties and voluntary associations that are independent of the government. These organizations can have a variety of goals and can compete in elections.[10]

In practice, Lebanon is not a full-fledged Western-type democracy for it does not meet all of the above criteria. Unrestricted freedom of speech, organization, and dissent are lacking. However, formal statements by officials may paint a different picture. Most critical for stable democracies is the presence of civil society. "Civil society" refers to the social groupings that mediate between government agencies and primary groups such as individuals and families. Many years ago, renowned sociologist Durkheim recognized the indispensable role of civil society, or what he termed "secondary groups," in integrating a nation:

> A nation can be maintained only if, between the state and the individual, there is intercalated a whole series of secondary groups near enough to the individuals to attract them strongly in their sphere of action and drag them, in this way, into the torrent of social life.[11]

In a Western democracy, these intermediary units—such as nongovernmental organizations (NGOs), labor syndicates, and political parties—are characterized by: "(1) independence from state institutions as well as primary units, (2) self-organization and a corporate status that is organized and protected by the state, and (3) the capacity to govern their members."[12] Lebanon has a large number of NGOs and private corporations, which made civil society stronger than the government during the years of strife. However, like other Arab societies, the Lebanese civil society is not run democratically, but is "dominated by traditions of familial and sectarian loyalty."[13] Furthermore, a crucial feature that is missing from many agencies of Lebanese civil society is their autonomy from the state. Without a fully developed civil society and a democratic political culture, Lebanon is unlikely to become fully democratic in the Western sense.[14]

As Hudson once remarked, Lebanon is stable enough to attract investments, now more than before the end of the civil war in 1990. The main source of stability is the prevalence of security. Maintenance of security is the most important goal proclaimed by the government. In former President Hrawi's words, "security comes before bread." Much of the government's efforts, and that of Syria too, are concentrated on that goal. So far, these efforts have been very successful, and many people seem to support that goal. When students at the Lebanese University were asked to name three major obligations that the government has towards citizens, the most important obligation named was security (51%). Therefore, it is no longer accurate to assume that a radio speech or even a bloody confrontation between the police force and protesting demonstrators would generate popular upheaval.

Hudson's statement concerning reform and corruption continues to be relevant. Stories of corruption in government agencies are public knowledge. Hariri publicly admitted his failure to reform the government bureaucracy.[15] Cabinet crises still occur as they did in pre-war Lebanon, but their nature is altered. In the past, the conflict was between the premier and the president. Now that the president's powers are curtailed and the speaker of parliament has assumed new powers, the premier is sometimes at odds with the president and at other times with the speaker of parliament. Periodically, disputes rage between any two of the ruling triumvirate known in Lebanon as the "troika." As a result, operations at some public agencies and/or the parliament become paralyzed, raising doubts about the durability and strength of cooperation among the leaders of the three major religious sects.

The party system that was feeble in the 1960s and early 1970s is now virtually dead. The party system that exists in Western democracies does not exist in Lebanon. National secular parties that were active before and during the civil war have either shrunk to small numbers, or have grown so weak that their presence on the ground is no longer felt.[16] What does exist instead are either the traditional factional formations that have always marked Lebanese politics, or the recently-constituted Islamic fundamentalist groups and parties. Factional groups are composed of local notables, their clan, members of their village, town, or city, and business associates and clients. A coalition of factions generates electoral lists and parliamentary blocs. Members of a bloc usually agree to take the same position on issues under consideration by the chamber of deputies.[17] Islamic groups, notably, Hizbullah, are organized units that usually have explicit political agendas, yet offer a diversity of social services to their constituency, both members and nonmembers. Presently, elected members of Hizbullah form a separate bloc in the parliament, but they ran in the elections in coalition with other parties, factions, and individuals. The Hizbullah party draws significant support from the Shiite students in high schools and colleges, notably, the Lebanese University.

In describing pre-war Lebanon, Halim Barakat argued that its diverse groups live on the same territory, yet they differ on fundamentals. The Lebanese have no consensus over such fundamentals as the "National Pact, confessionalism, and...national identity."[18] Power is distributed unevenly among the religious groups, who tend to favor their own interests to that of the public. Open dialogue is missing among the different religious communities that are also geographically segregated.[19]

There were indications well before 1989 that the majority of the Lebanese from the various religious sects had reached a consensus on few political principles. They had agreed that Lebanon should remain a sovereign independent state within its 1943 borders, that no sect is reducible by force, and no party can impose its will or agenda on the others by violent means.[20] The plight of the Lebanese convinced a large segment of Arabs to accept the existence of Lebanon within its 1943 borders and the Lebanese national identity.[21]

Consensus on some of the fundamental issues that divided the Lebanese was reached in 1989 with the signing of the National Unity Document/Covenant, also known as the Taif accord. The decades-long debate on the national identity of Lebanon was finally settled. According to the Taif agreement, Lebanon is an independent sovereign Arab state, whose national identity is Arab, as is its destiny. The accord affirms that Lebanon is neither a temporary arrangement that will eventually give way to a larger entity (such as Greater Syria or Arab nation-state), nor a Western preserve, but a "final homeland" to all its citizens. Apparently, this critical principle of the accord has received an overwhelming support from various parties in Lebanon, including those who rejected the whole accord. Still, the Lebanese do not share a common interpretation of their history, a necessary factor for developing a stable political entity

Disagreement on the 1943 National Pact, another disputed fundamental, has also been resolved. The Pact, a temporary verbal understanding between the leaders of the two main religious communities, has been replaced by the Taif accord. Unlike the old pact, the new accord is a permanent written document that supplements the French-inspired constitution of 1926. Nevertheless, some of the main principles in the National Pact are now affirmed in the new accord, notably, the sectarian allocation of top positions in the political system and public administration. Regardless of probable demographic changes in the future, which may alter the relative sizes of the various religious groups, the president should always be a Maronite Christian, the Premier a Sunni Muslim, and the speaker of parliament a Shiite Muslim. In other words, the three largest confessional groups have agreed, at least for the foreseeable future, that the allocation of political power should not be linked to their population size, thereby undermining the foundation of the 1943 political formula.

Furthermore, article 95 of the 1926 constitution, which deals with sectarianism, was amended in 1990. The new version reads:

> The parliament...will take appropriate measures to bring about an end to political sectarianism on the basis of a plan which will advance in stages, establishing a national council...to consider and recommend appropriate measures for the cancellation of sectarianism.... During the transitional period: (a) the different sects will be fairly represented in the cabinet, and (b) the principle of sectarian representation in employment (i.e., in public positions) will be canceled and specialization and qualifications will be adopted instead as criteria for employment except in cases of employees in the First Category who will be selected on an equal basis from among Christians and Muslims.[22]

No national council, as of yet, has been formed to design such a plan, and the principle of sectarian allocation of public positions continues to prevail. Despite recurrent calls by prominent politicians for the abolition of sectarianism in state bureaucracy, the daily practices and cabinet decisions have proven otherwise. Not only should government appointees belong to particular sects to meet specified confessional quotas, but they must also prove their personal loyalty to the chief representative of their sect in the political regime. For the three major religious groups, the patron is the President, Prime Minister, or Speaker of Parliament. The other religious communities have other known patrons. This should come as no surprise since the patronage system prevails in various parts of the Arab world. It is common in politics, business, extended family, parochial associations, and even in voluntary associations that assume a modern appearance.

Religion

Religion is one of the basic enduring components of the Lebanese social structure. Rather than being a mere spiritual force, it is institutionalized on denominational lines such that each religious sect has its own courts, traditions, social, economic, and for some groups political organizations. When Lebanon was under Ottoman rule, the "millet system" classified Ottoman subjects according to their religious sect. Muslims and Christians of various confessions became aware of their distinctiveness because it carried with it certain political and social obligations. European colonialist states nurtured this sectarian distinctiveness through a variety of means: educational missionaries, military and financial support, and political protection for individual religious sects. The sect thus became an important social entity even after the end of the French mandate on Lebanon. As aptly put by the noted historian Albert Hourani:

> The sect persisted as a social entity even after the impulse which gave it birth died away. To leave one's sect was to leave one's whole world, and to live without loyalties, the protections of a community, the consciousness of solidarity and the comfort of normality.[23]

Lebanon has eighteen religious sects that are officially recognized by the state. Article 9 of the 1926 constitution, which deals with religious freedom, remains in force:

> Freedom of belief is absolute, and the state in rendering homage to the Most High, respects all religions and creeds and guarantees the freedom

of exercising religious rites under its protection provided that this does not disturb public order, and it guarantees to people in their various millets respect of laws of personal status and religious interests.[24]

Religious courts of various sects continue to apply their own laws of personal status involving marriage contracts, divorce, baptism, adoption, and inheritance. All attempts to take this privilege away from religious authorities have been firmly rebuffed by both the clergy and prominent politicians, especially among Sunni and Shiite Muslims. A noted example is Hrawi's recent proposal to introduce civil marriage as an available option for those who desire it. So far, couples from different religious sects, who are prohibited by their religious authorities to wed, travel to neighboring states, usually Cyprus, to obtain marriage certificates from a civil court.

During the years of turmoil, 1975-1990, sectarian feelings and practice reached their zenith. There was an increase in the number of welfare associations, educational and research institutions, commercial establishments, and political groupings that were organized along confessional lines. Generally speaking, in wartime and in the absence of the state, citizens are expected to seek refuge in their parochial communities and find solace in their kinship and confessional ties. But when war ends and the state regains its lost power, state supporters have a weaker rationale for maintaining sectarian-based institutions. Furthermore, as the national state asserts its authority, one would expect its citizens' drive to build and expand sectarian organizations to ebb.

On the contrary, the sectarian élan remains as strong as ever. The rise in confessionally based associations has not receded or subsided. The organizations that were born during the war years as small, uncertain projects have either gained legal status or are lobbying to attain it. A number of religious leaders of the major religious sects now run their own universities or colleges of higher education.[25]

A few years ago, a sincere, yet limited dialogue started among representatives of different religious communities. The committee for Muslim-Christian Dialogue has been working relentlessly toward that goal, but the obstacles are huge, particularly the lack of trust among the various sectarian leaders. One noteworthy illustration is the communiqué of the synod "for the sake of Lebanon," a meeting of the Maronite clergy that was sponsored by the Vatican in December 1995. This communiqué called for the "departure of Syrian forces," emphasizing Lebanon's "cultural pluralism" and "consensual democracy."

The wording and timing of this document aroused the anger of both Sunni and Shiite religious and political leaders. The Shiite Imam, Shamsuddin, stressed that Lebanon is a "single political society," while the Sunni Mufti, Qabbani, criticized the use of the terms "consensual democracy," which to him meant veto power of the sects, and thus a negation of national unity. The dialogue committee, whose members were present on site when the communiqué was issued in the Vatican, eventually succeeded to defuse the tension between the Maronite patriarch and his two Muslim counterparts. The Pope's visit to Lebanon in May 1997 also contributed to the further reduction of the tension. The Pope's speeches aimed at promoting a reconciliation between Muslims and Christians and convincing them that the prosperity of Lebanon is contingent on their mutual understanding and peaceful coexistence.

In the early 1970s, Barakat found religious communities to be geographically segregated. During the civil strife, their segregation was accentuated. With an explicit or implicit policy of religious cleansing by the warring factions, most communities attained a high degree of religious homogeneity. In many villages and urban quarters, one would find the more extreme form of sectarian homogeneity. As a result, it was feasible to estimate the numbers of Muslims and Christians in most local provinces (known as *qadas*) in 1988.[26] However, there is an observed decline in geographic segregation since the end of the war in 1990. Many people who fled religiously-mixed neighborhoods during the war have returned to their original domiciles, and many newly weds are taking up residence in suburbs that are not inhabited by co-religionists. Still, the extent of geographic segregation of religious communities is more pronounced today than it had been before the onset of the war.

Undoubtedly, political sectarianism has had many advocates within and without the political system. Seeking to keep their sect dominant, most Maronite politicians before and during the civil war vehemently opposed any change in the "delicate political system," ruling out the viability of any non-confessional alternative to Lebanese politics.[27] It is the opinion of this author that these arguments lost credence during the horrific years of strife that wrecked the country. Members of parliament, the guardians of the sectarian system, finally agreed to change Article 95 of the constitution, thereby pledging to end political sectarianism through a gradual process. "To many, this was too small of a reward compared with the amount of suffering and bloodshed that went on for sixteen years of fighting,"[28] parliamentarians added. In postwar Lebanon, many of the incidents of corruption, embezzlement, and incompetence in public agencies are related to the institution of sectarianism, nepotism, and parochialism in administrative bureaucracy. Furthermore, sectarianism in public administration does not exist in a pure form separate from parochialism, patronage (*wasta*), and familism. The historical experience of public employment in Lebanon shows that sectarian practices and kinship allegiance have often contributed to the prevailing corruption, ineffectiveness, and inefficiency in public agencies.

At the level of sociological theory, the characteristics of "bureaucracy" that Max Weber introduced are at odds with the practices of nepotism, parochialism, and patronage. In a fully bureaucratic system, officials perform their duties in a strictly objective and professional manner regardless of their personal relations, emotional feelings, beliefs, and prejudices. Weber adds:

> The more complex and specialized modern culture becomes, the more its external apparatus demands replacement of the traditional lord, capable of being moved through personal sympathy, goodwill, mercy, or gratitude, with a personally unsympathetic and, therefore, strictly 'objective' expert.[29]

Although the same major religious communities that existed before the war have maintained their presence, their political power in relation to one another has been altered. The war and the Taif accord primarily caused this change. Christian Maronites are no longer uncontestably the most powerful in politics. Their power has receded in the face of new political actors among the other religious communities. On the other hand, within each religious community, new social classes and political leaders have emerged either as rivals or replacements to the old classes and political elites.

Among the Sunnis, Hariri stands for new, aggressive, and innovative political and economic power that has dwarfed traditional leaders and their heirs, evoking their indignation and hatred. Heirs of leading politicians include Tammam Salam of Beirut, Omar Karami of Tripoli, and Mustafa Sa'ad of Saida. The only non-traditional politician who, to some extent, continues to challenge Hariri's leadership is former Prime Minister Salim Hoss. In the 1996 parliamentary elections, Hoss garnered the second highest number of votes in Beirut after Hariri.

Capitalizing on the extensive social, charitable services and educational loans (de facto fellowships) that his organizations have provided since the early 1980s, Hariri managed to acquire a substantial popular base among the various religious groups, particularly Sunnis. He has also benefited from the enhanced authority of the premiership under the Taif accord to create a new image for a Prime Minister. As Prime Minister, Hariri is not a first minister in a cabinet headed by a president as in pre-war Lebanon, but rather a ruler among two other equals: the president and the speaker of parliament. In many events, Hariri proved the strongest and most capable statesman of the ruling triumvirate.[30]

The Shiites have the Speaker of Parliament, Nabih Berri, and spokespersons and principal cadres of Hizbullah as their new political elite. They have virtually ended the traditional leaderships of the As'ad and Hamadeh clans and weakened the influence of the Husseinis. As the head of the popular mass Shiite movement, *Amal*, Berri easily rose to power. In the same manner, the leaders of the cohesive, para-military, ideological party Hizbullah were able to get elected to the parliament through the efforts of their party members. The historical longstanding strong influence of the Osseiran clan in the South has declined despite their alliance with Berri. Unlike the Sunnis, the Shiite political elite shares power with the clergy, notably, Imam Muhammad Mahdi Shamsuddin, head of the Islamic Shiite Higher Council, and the Islamic scholar, Muhammad Hussein Fadlullah. Both have proved indispensable foci for mass mobilization among the Shiites.

Unlike the other sects, the Maronites suffer most from a vacuum in leadership.[31] The traditional political leaderships of the Gemayyels, Sham'ouns, and Eddehs have been emasculated. Raymond Eddeh and former President Amin Gemayyel live in exile. Dani Sham'oun lacks the personal charisma that his father had as well as extensive Maronite support. Ironically, Hrawi and Maronite politicians of the current regime did not make the list of the most liked leaders in the student survey. Instead, the Maronites have General Michel Aoun as the new exiled leader of popular dissent, whose popularity among Maronite students was evident in the 1996 survey.

Oddly enough, the resident leadership among Maronites has been filled not by politicians, but by Cardinal Sfeir, the head of the Maronite church. Despite backing the Taif accord, Sfeir has persistently voiced the Maronites' grievances regarding alleged discrimination against them by the government, Lebanon's "loss of sovereignty" due to the Syrian military presence, and "improper" implementation of the Taif accord.

Maronite opposition to the regime has coined a new term in local political vocabulary namely *ihbat*, or subdued and depressed, to describe the state the Maronites are allegedly in.   Several Maronite politicians and clergymen have developed a habit of using this term in various situations. Apparently, many Maronites remain unable to envision a Lebanon they do not dominate.[32]

Among the Orthodox Christians, Najah Wakim and Michel Murr represent the sect's new political elite. Wakim is an outspoken opponent of the regime, particularly of Hariri. His opposition stems from his assessment of Hariri's economic and social policy, which in his view favors the rich. Murr, on the other hand, is one of the pillars of the present regime and among the wealthiest in the country.

The Druze leadership in postwar Lebanon reveals the persistence of old patterns in a new guise. The Junblati-Yazbaki split among the Druze remains pronounced, but today's representatives are the young sons of the late traditional feudal lords. Walid Junblat, son of the late Kamal Junblat, has inherited his father's roles as tribal chief and head of the Druze-dominant Progressive Socialist Party. In addition to these roles, Junblat is part of the current regime as a minister and member of parliament. He is a controversial figure who evokes mixed feelings among people. Talal Arslan, son of the late Majid Arslan, has succeeded his father as head of the Arslan clan, or Yazbakis, and is now a member of both the cabinet and parliament.

In addition to the shifting of political power among religious communities, economic power has changed as well. Big business establishments in services, which constitute the main vital economic sector in Lebanon, are owned and managed by individuals and families from the various sects. Many of the owners made their fortunes in Africa and Latin America, while others have amassed their wealth from the people's misery during the war. The long-claimed underprivileged Shiites now have economically powerful members. On the prestigious "trade and industry" executive board sits the ultra rich of the various religious communities. Business contracts for reconstruction and rehabilitation of public buildings, infrastructure and services go to contractors from different sects, yet most of them are supporters or friends of one or more of the ruling triumvirate.

Education

The French mandate has left a lasting mark on the education system of Lebanon. Shortly after occupying the country, the French formulated the 1926 constitution which included the following article (Article 10) on educational freedom:

> Education shall be free provided it does not disturb public order or violate morals, or impinge on the dignity of any religion or sect. The rights of communities to maintain their own private schools cannot be diminished provided they conform with the general regulation issued by the state in the field of public instruction.[33]

The French were keen on maintaining an atmosphere of educational freedom dominated by private schools, particularly those run by foreign missionaries. They promoted their language and civilization through French missionary schools, and designed a curriculum to their liking in public schools. However, there was at least one educational system that challenged their hegemony and prevented them from fully dominating the education system: the Anglo-Saxon (American and British) approach.

This French legacy remains strong, yet seriously challenged by both American and national outlooks to education. Today, most schools, both public and private, continue to teach French as a second language. Within the private sector, the majority of students in foreign schools are Christians. The extent of religious polarization is extreme in French missionaries. However, the proportion of Muslims in American schools is either equal to or greater than that of Christians. In public schools, the overwhelming majority of students are Muslims.[34]

Before the war, religion was taught in public schools by appointees of religious authorities of the various sects. A member of a denomination taught children from that denomination. This meant that Shiite Muslim children, for example, were taught by a Shiite clergyman and did not attend lessons on Christianity. One can easily predict the likely adverse effects of such a system on national unity and inter-confessional cooperation and understanding. In practice, however, this system was rarely implemented, for appointees were sent instead to their own private sectarian schools, partly because of a shortage of teachers of religion. In private schools, students received religious instruction in the confession of the school owners. Accordingly, Shiite Islamic schools today, for instance, teach the Shiite strand of Islam, while Catholic schools teach Catholicism.[35]

Social studies textbooks vary in content depending on the religious affiliation of the school administration. Biased material and indoctrination mark the textbooks. For example, books taught in Islamic schools refer to the Arabs as "our brothers" and emphasize the role of Muslim heroes in history. In contrast, Christian schools highlight the Phoenician origin of Lebanon and praise Phoenician historical figures like Hannibal. Furthermore, the time allocated to each topic within the social studies subject varies from one school to another. For example, one school may allocate three periods to discuss Arab nationalism while another may just mention it in passing. This suggests "a strong relationship between social studies education and religious conflict between the Christian and Muslim communities."[36]

Family and Kinship

Despite their importance to the Lebanese, sectarian loyalties do not supersede family ties. The building block of the Lebanese society is the family. The family is the principal pillar of social structure. Undoubtedly it is the most important social institution with which people identify. The influence of the family on the life of the individual surpasses all other institutions including the state. The whole family shares one's successes or failures and is held accountable to one's transgressions and sins.

Traditionally, the Lebanese family is patrilineal and patriarchal. The head is the male elder, or the lord (*rab al-usrah*). His wife is subordinate; she is linked, (*qarina*) or tied (*aqila*), to him for he is usually the economic provider.[37] Family members are bound by strong emotional feelings of mutual support that demand unswerving loyalty to this primary group. Members often endure economic hardship and sacrifice their time and comfort to help, protect, and please siblings, parents, children, and kin. Such bonds are extended to parochial units such as city neighborhoods, villages, and towns of residence or birth. In villages and small towns, one's neighbors are often one's kin. Even in cities, members of the same extended family or clan live in close proximity to one another.

In the past, endogamy was common in the Lebanese extended family. It was preferable for girls to wed their first cousins, or else their kin. In the period 1967-1969, Lebanese anthropologist Fuad Khuri found that 11% of the marriages among Muslims in the southern suburb of

Beirut were between first cousins (*bint 'am* marriage). In Khuri's study, all endogamous marriages accounted for 38% of the total marriages.[38] Today, endogamy is observed to be on the decline, but no recent statistics are available.

The family as an organization and value system is closely related to the other major social institutions in Lebanon namely religion and state. This interrelationship is embodied in Hisham Sharabi's concept of "neopatriarchy" that refers to both macrostructures (such as state and economy) and microstructures (such as individuals and primary groups). Neopatriarchy is the end product of social change that patriarchal societies undergo under conditions of economic dependency on capitalist superpowers. It is neither authentically traditional nor fully modern and has many aspects: political, social, economic, and cultural. The father (patriarch) is dominant whether in politics or primordial relations. Only vertical relations exist between the patriarch—be he a father in a family, a state ruler, or a company CEO—and his dependents.[39]

As in other Arab countries, the prevailing neopatriarchal family in Lebanon reinforces the larger system of patronage in society. This system uses *wasta,* or mediation, a practice developed in the family. The process of appointment to public positions, for instance, requires the mediation of at least one influential politician or notable who would recommend the candidate to the selection committee or head of the public agency. The Lebanese child is socialized to *wasta* as a conflict resolution mechanism.[40] For example, when a child fights with a sibling over some personal belongings (playing with one's toy), he/she usually seeks the intervention of a mediator (a parent, an older sibling, or elder kin) who has the power to settle the dispute.

Family values and practices are often brought to the work setting. The concept of "public office" is radically different from that used in western countries. The Arab scholar, Abdullah Laroui, provides an accurate description:

> Public office [is] a privilege rather than a position of public service. Official relations are based on charity and loyalty...and the public officials' behavior is determined by private concerns in dealing with individuals who seek their official services.[41]

For a typical public officer, the workplace "is no more than an extension of the place of sociability and relaxation.... Guests are received and entertained, coffee or tea served, and amiable conversation enjoyed at leisure."[42] When discharging duties, personal and family interests of the public officer always come before public or institutional interests. One's performance at work goes unnoticed because recognition requires personal connections and "proper backing rather than competence, efficiency, hard work, or sacrifice."[43] In stark contrast to Khalaf's praise for primordial ties and confessional bureaucracy, Sharabi pinpoints the deleterious effects of familism, factionalism, and sectarianism: "Patronage...generates egoism and cynicism as it reinforces the system of obedience, passivity, and submission."[44]

While the neopatriarchal family form is thought to prevail in Lebanon, there are powerful signs of its decline in favor of a modern democratic form, as shall be elaborated in chapter 5. Despite the paucity of data, the Lebanese family must have undergone significant changes in structure and function as a result of the civil war, rapid urbanization, expansion of the educational system, shifting economic activities from agriculture toward the services industry, and globalization of economy and culture. One indicator of this change is the decline in the percentage of extended families. The recent survey of housing and population in 1996 shows that the overwhelming majority of Lebanese families (78%) are of the nuclear type (i.e., a family made up of parents and dependent children). In the past, a high proportion of families were extended (i.e., parents, children and other kin sharing the same accommodation). Other more important changes in the internal dynamics of the family are inferred from the empirical findings of this study.

External Powers

Five external powers have a significant bearing on Lebanon's politics and society: the U.S., France, Israel, Syria, Iran, and Saudi Arabia. Like any other small developing country, Lebanon is strongly influenced by the economic and political changes in its region (the Middle East) and the world at large. With the demise of the Soviet Union as a superpower, the U.S. has become the sole political and military superpower and it remains the largest economic power. In the Middle East, Arab states and organizations that relied on the former Soviet Union for military and political support in their conflict with Israel have turned to the U.S., seeking its brokerage of a peaceful settlement. As a result, the political role of the U.S. in the Arab world, including Lebanon, became prominent.

As the peace process proceeded after the Madrid meetings in 1992, pan-Arab, socialists, and other revolutionary ideologies and parties were immensely debilitated. The only national cause that most Lebanese support today is ending the Israeli occupation of southern Lebanon. The means need not be violent, as Lebanon demands the unconditional withdrawal of Israeli forces in return for guaranteeing security for the bordering areas. However, the military action by Hizbullah and other para-military groups that target the occupied zone has been condoned by the government and supported by many people. More generally, the role of Israel in Lebanon is perceived as adversarial, threatening internal peace and economic prosperity.

France has played a primary role in Lebanon's politics and educational system since its mandate years, which lasted until the civil war broke out in 1975. During the war, France's role shrank considerably but has since revived during the wake of the war. Today, France is an important player in Lebanon's domestic politics and society. However, the nature of its role has shifted from being a protector of the Maronites to that of a supporter for the sovereignty and independence of the state of Lebanon with all its religious communities. France is now a key participant in the reconstruction projects of Lebanon and a primary consultant in cultural activities and educational programs.

The 1991 Gulf war and its aftermath further weakened cooperation among Arab states. The Arab League, the only regional organization that stands for pan-Arab solidarity and interests, is ineffective and aging. Meetings of the league have turned into a show of disunity and discord. Arab politics is atomized, with each state placing its domestic interests before pan-Arab concerns. A host of interstate disputes continue to mark the region.[45] Within this atmosphere of Arab disarray, Lebanon developed unique relations with neighboring Syria, whose army played a decisive role in ending the civil war. The political and military role of Syria in Lebanon continues to rally the support of most people, particularly Muslims. However, many Maronites and other Christians repeatedly voice opposition to the Syrian role and military presence in Lebanon, notably, the head of the Maronite church, Cardinal Sfeir. In addition to the Syrian army, a large unknown number of Syrian civilians work in Lebanon as skilled and unskilled laborers. Lebanese workers have not welcomed these Syrian laborers as they accept lower salaries with no social or health benefits, thereby giving them a competitive edge. Syrian workers are also willing to perform menial jobs, which Lebanese workers may be reluctant to do.

In addition to Syria, Iran is another external power that has a significant weight in Lebanese political and social affairs—its influence mainly felt through Hizbullah. The Iranian Islamic revolution has left its mark on the Shiite religious, social, and political life. For example, many Shiite women took to wearing the veil, following in the footsteps of their Iranian counterparts. Even the type of veil many women wear is Iranian-style as opposed to the Syrian, Saudi, or traditional Lebanese style. Through Iranian financial support, Hizbullah has managed to establish social welfare institutions, schools, and hospitals that cater to their needy and poor constituency, many of whom are not Shiites.

Since Hariri assumed the position of Prime Minister, the Saudi political and economic role in Lebanon has grown. The Saudis have demonstrated their support for him and confidence in his leadership by investing in Lebanon and providing grants and loans to reconstruction projects. The other Arab Gulf countries, notably, Kuwait, followed suit. Today, Arab Gulf states and their citizens are active investors in the country's economic projects.

Summary

A host of changes in social structure have occurred in Lebanon since the early seventies. Tens of thousands died as a result of the war and a lot more emigrated or were displaced from their homes to other regions within the country. Consequently, the geographic distribution of the population by *muhafaza* has changed while maintaining geographic segregation of religious groups. Economically, despite impressive achievements in reconstruction and stabilization of the local currency, Lebanon's rate of growth has slowed down, the budget deficit and national debt have both increased, and the rift between the rich and the poor has widened.

The political system, presumably democratic, suffers from restricted freedom of speech and organization, and inefficiency and corruption mar the state bureaucracy. The civil society is dominated by sectarian and familial loyalty, and all political parties but Hizbullah are feeble. However, the Lebanese now agree on their national identity and on the sectarian allocation of the top positions in the political system.

The family in Lebanon remains neopatriarchal in nature, but there are signs of a shift toward a more democratic form. As for the role of external powers, the study identifies five powers that have a significant bearing on Lebanon's politics and society: the U.S., France, Israel, Syria, Iran, and Saudi Arabia.

CHAPTER 5

SOCIAL VALUES: BETWEEN TRADITION AND POSTMODERNITY

> Individualization is a paradoxical compulsion for the
> construction, self-design and self-staging of not just
> one's own biography, but also its commitments and
> networks as preferences and life phases change.
>
> Ulrich Beck[1]

This chapter investigates the prevalence of a set of individual values among Lebanese college students. The definition and measurement of five of these values—individualism, authoritarianism, equalitarianism, internal control, and fatalism—are drawn from previous studies in the West. Six others—*asabiya*, face saving, form-content, shame-guilt, group work, and manual work—refer to stereotypic, Orientalists' views of Arab culture that have been propounded by influential Western authors. Some of these six values are measured using statements made by Raphael Patai in his widely read book, *The Arab Mind*. Measurement of the remaining values is based on some ideas and phrases from Halim Barakat's book, *The Arab World*.

The personal values examined may reflect certain societal values, which in turn can explain themes and observations presented in earlier chapters. Included in the statistical analysis of the data are socioeconomic determinants and correlates of the students' values. Two statistical techniques of multivariate analysis are employed: analysis of variance and logistic regression. The former is used when the dependent variable (i.e. social value or norm) is continuous, while the latter is used when the dependent variable is dichotomous (can assume either 0 or 1 as a score). Since the statistics generated by applying these methods are not known to most readers outside academia, they will not be presented in the chapter but are placed in Appendix A. Yet, the results of the statistical analysis will be presented in simplified terms. Instead of ANOVA tables, simple statistical measures like means, medians, and t values are provided.

The data were collected from students at AUB in the spring of 1996 and at LU in the fall of 1996 using the same survey instrument. However, the original questionnaire distributed to AUB students was in English, and the one given to LU students was an Arabic translation.[2] The data set analyzed is a combination of the responses from both universities.

Individualism

Individualism is defined as "the principle or habit or belief in independent thought or action...the pursuit of individual rather than common or collective interests."[3] The doctrine of individualism assumed different elements in different historical eras. In the eighteenth and nineteenth centuries, this doctrine highlighted "the centrality of a self-representing individual,"[4] who is responsible for his actions and decisions. This version later gave way to another, that of "the self-expressing individual" where "all interests are ultimately interests of the bare individual."[5] Rather than emphasize self-control and hard work, the new version puts a premium on freedom of choice in politics, economy, and personal life. The individual is conceived as an end; the ultimate objective is self-actualization and self-fulfillment despite the existence of a constraining social structure.

Sociologist Robert Bellah and associates describe individualism in terms such as hedonism, utilitarianism, competition, self-reliance, personal freedom, equality, competence, independence from family and church, and loneliness.[6] They lament the sway of individualism over American society, viewing it as a crisis.

Diametrically opposed to individualism is the notion of "collectivism," which emphasizes the prevailing views and goals of the group rather than the self. In a collectivist culture, social norms, not self-interests, guide one's social behavior.[7] Several social scientists contend that collectivists strongly consider "the implications of their actions for others...feel susceptible to social influence, are very concerned with their self-presentation and saving face, and feel that their lives are involved in the lives of others."[8]   Comparable contrasts between individualism and collectivism were drawn by classical sociologists using different terms. Durkheim distinguished between "mechanic solidarity" and "organic solidarity." Tonnies separated the notion of *gemeinschaft* (community) from that of *gesellschaft* (society). Weber contrasted "associative" with "communal" organization.

Individualism is measured using the following three statements with which respondents can either agree or disagree:

- A person should always be the master of his own fate.
- A man must make his own decisions, uninfluenced by the opinions of others.
- A man can learn better by striking out boldly on his own than he can by following the advice of others.[9]

A three-point index of individualism was constructed from these statements, with 0 as lower bound and 3 as upper bound. On average, students scored 2.05 and half of them scored 2.00 or above (median=2.00).   Hence, most students had a propensity toward individualism rather than collectivism, and more than a third (36%) agreed with all three statements obtaining the highest score of 3.00 (table 5.1).   In the World Value Survey of 1990, a similar, though not equivalent, three-point index of cultural individualism had a mean of 1.90 for all Western countries combined.[10]   In other words, on average, Lebanese students are similar to Westerners with regard to individualistic beliefs.

Individualism bears a statistically significant association with six variables combined: sex, university, academic major, father's occupation, mother's education, and parents' place of residence (table A1). Surprisingly, the mean value of the index of individualism is higher among females than males (table 5.2). In other words, female students believed in individualism more strongly than males even though they are more closely-knit to the primary social groups to which they belong. Their belief could have stemmed from the greater demand which society places on women as opposed to men. It is equally likely that some female students could have developed these beliefs as a result of observing and living with independent mothers.

The long years of turmoil have taught the Lebanese women a great deal about survival and independence since the male guardians, whom they have grown to depend on, could no longer provide financial or physical security. Many of them saw their hopes crushed when their husbands, fathers, or brothers were either killed, maimed, or forced to travel in order to seek work. Such a situation opened their eyes to a new reality: one in which they had to fight their life battles alone and find their own niche in society. Even when men were present, the security situation was so bad at times that they were forced to stay away from home until the situation calmed down. This left women alone in charge of the household sometimes for days.

One likely consequence of individualistic values is a rise in individualistic behavior among female students, a phenomenon that has already surfaced among adult women in the larger society. Signs of individualistic behavior in the form of assertive action and independence are plentiful in postwar Lebanon. On college campuses, girls are competing fiercely with boys in various academic disciplines, outsmarting them in many cases. In work settings, adult women are proving equal to men in terms of qualifications and work ethics. Women who have assumed senior positions are usually very competent and self-actualized and have won the respect of male workers, be they subordinates, superiors, or colleagues.[11]

Within the conjugal family, wives are so actively engaging in decision making that no action on virtually all major issues is taken without their consent. Undoubtedly, the new styles of childrearing that Lebanese parents have used in the recent past have contributed to this finding. Gone are the days when baby girls were raised to feel and act inferior to baby boys.

Contrary to mainstream opinion and research results in other societies, which claim a positive, monotonic relationship between a mother's education and indicators of modernity, this study shows a different relationship. Students whose mothers have a low level of education (completed intermediate education or lower) or a high level of education (completed college) have significantly higher levels of individualism than those whose mothers have a medium level of education (completed secondary education) (table 5.2). This relationship remains significant after controlling for a variety of other background variables: mother's occupation, father's education and occupation, religion, religiosity, place of residence, major, sex, and nature of closest group. An explanation for this result did not appear in the data and, therefore, a theoretical rationale could not be found. There are probably

Table 5.1: Social Values of Lebanese Students, 1996

Value	Minimum	Maximum	Mean	Median	Standard Deviation	No. of Valid Cases
Authoritarianism	0 (24%)	3	1.108	1.00	.814	1601
Individualism	0	3 (36%)	2.046	2.00	.878	1619
Internal Control	0	4 (24%)	2.788	3.00	.934	1600
Fatalism	0 (12%)	4	1.948	2.00	1.185	1589
Equalitarianism	0	1 (80%)	0.800	1.00	.400	1649
Asabiyah	0 (58%)	1	0.417	0.00	.493	1637
Dislike of Group Work	0 (42%)	2	0.767	1.00	.738	1637
Form-Content	0 (16%)	2	1.343	2.00	.735	1617
Shame-Guilt	0 (36%)	3	0.993	1.00	.904	1620
Dislike of Manual Work	0 (48%)	3	0.707	1.00	.794	1627
Face Saving	0 (11%)	3	1.550	2.00	.864	1617

some attributes about those secondary educated women that account for their different behavior from the other women. Factors such as age, childrearing style, or war experience are suggested as possible causes for this variation. In-depth interviews with a sample of these women could prove useful. A comparison of the mean values of individualism for LU and AUB students (table 5.2) shows that LU students believe in individualism more strongly than AUB students. A combined effect of social background and academic setting may account for this difference. Compared to LU students, AUB students come from more advantaged social backgrounds; their parents tend to be more educated, wealthier, and more sophisticated urbanites. In addition, the administrative structures and academic practices at LU and AUB are quite different. Instructors offer little help and rarely interact with students on a daily basis. An AUB student, by contrast, expects a lot from the instructor besides lecturing, including follow-ups, feedbacks, and regular interaction during class and office hours.[12]

Relevant research in other countries shows contradictory findings concerning the relation between social class and individualism. Some studies cite higher levels of individualism in the upper classes while other studies cite lower levels.[13] In this research, students from lower or middle social classes have a stronger inclination toward individualism than those from upper classes. Children of self-employed and professional parents are somewhat more individualistic than children of skilled workers or clerical and sales employees. Least individualistic are children of big business owners and managers (table 5.2).

Apparently, professionals and self-employed parents whose occupational success requires independent decisions and action have instilled similar values in their children. These parents tend to belong to the middle class and, therefore, live in an unstable status from which they could either fall to the lower class or move up to the upper class. Such a situation requires especially hard work and individualistic values in order to maintain or improve their social status. Rich business executives and owners, on the other hand, seem to have given their children the impression that independence of mind and action does not always pay off. It is common knowledge that social networks and parochial ties rather than individual labor have led to the rise and continuity of prominent commercial establishments in Lebanon and other Arab countries. Such an experience might have diluted in children of big business owners and managers the belief in individualism.

Table 5.2: Mean of Individualism by Sex, University, Major, Father's
Occupation, Mother's Education, and Parents' Place of Residence

Variable			Category	N	Mean
	Sex		Male	510	1.89
			Female	800	2.12
	University		Lebanese	741	2.13
			American	569	1.90
	Major		Engineering & Agriculture	165	2.07
			Medicine & Health Sciences	125	2.15
			Basic Sciences	247	2.11
			Humanities & Social Sciences	773	1.98
	Father's Occupation		Big Business Owner/Manager	187	1.94
			Small Business & Professional	508	2.07
			Employee & Worker	615	2.03
	Mother's Occupation		Below Secondary	509	2.09
			Secondary	443	1.91
			University	358	2.09
	Parents' Residence		Cities	886	1.98
			Other Areas-Rural	424	2.14

Grand Mean=1.11

A large percentage of LU students have rural as opposed to urban or city backgrounds. In a typical village, life is rough—the winters are cold, public services are limited, government centers are remote, and cash is scarce. These harsh realities of rural life make one's survival contingent on self-reliance, a value that is central to individualism. It is no wonder then that students whose parents reside in rural areas have more individualistic attitudes than those whose parents reside in cities (table 5.2).

The findings also reveal that the academic major plays a significant role in fostering individualistic values. Students majoring in languages, humanities, and social sciences are least individualistic, while medical and health science students are most individualistic (table 5.2). Part of this difference has to do with the nature of training and curriculum in the different academic disciplines. Humanities and social sciences deal with more abstract, romantic ideas and idealistic visions, espouse humanistic attitudes, and kindle students' interest in reform. These aspects of the major are more conducive to collectivism than individualism. By contrast, medical and health sciences deal with pragmatic decisions, realistic situations, and hard, empirical facts. These features engender individualistic values. In addition, the difference by major may also result from differential personal qualities between the students. Humanities and social sciences are overwhelmed with students who are less competitive than those in the medical and health sciences are. Competition among students in the medical and health sciences is fierce, beginning from the time they enter the school, and lasting until they graduate. This continuous competition undoubtedly nurtures their individualistic values.

Authoritarianism

Authoritarianism is a syndrome of personality characteristics. An authoritarian person exercises "complete or almost complete control over the will of another or of others."[14] An authoritarian attitude favors "complete obedience or subjection to authority as opposed to individual freedom."[15] Studies of authoritarianism began after World War II with the pioneering work of Theodor Adorno and his colleagues. In that work, the rise of Nazism in Europe was linked to the prevalence of authoritarian personalities that held extreme political views and rigid thinking.[16] Adorno developed a special scale to measure different aspects of authoritarianism.

In this study, a simplified measure of authoritarianism is used to tap the degree of obedience and respect for authority among students. A three-point index is constructed from the following three statements with which respondents can either agree or disagree:

- Disobeying an order is one thing you can't excuse.
- In any organization, if you lay down a rule, it must be obeyed and enforced.
- I rebel against an authority when I believe it is unjust.[17]

The index ranges from 0 to 3 where 3 is the upper bound indicating utmost respect and obedience for authority.

On average, students scored 1.11, which is lower than the mid-point of the index. Half the students scored below 1.00 (median=1.00), and a quarter scored 0 rejecting all three statements on authoritarianism (table 5.1). In other words, Lebanese students are closer to being rebellious than obedient to authority figures. Most do not consider the respect of rules and heeding orders as a *sine qua non* of organizations.

Authoritarianism is significantly related to four explanatory variables: sex, university, major, and parents' place of residence (table 5.3). A comparison of the mean value of the index of authoritarianism for males with that of females shows that females have less authoritarian values than males regardless of the other background variables (table A2). It seems that male authority is no longer a dreadful bogeyman to female students as women now perceive it in a new fashion. For instance, in the nuclear family, the image of the father has shifted from that of the omnipotent patriarch to that of the caring, supportive, older friend. In politics, rulers are no longer regarded as invincible, sacred personalities but rather as fallible individuals with limited capabilities. This result fits neatly with several other findings of this study: that women are more individualistic than men, less stereotypic about gender issues, and increasingly engaging in family decisions.

LU students have a stronger tendency toward authoritarianism than AUB students (table 5.3). Again, one can invoke differences in social background and academic setting to account for this finding: rural as opposed to urban background, lower rather than higher economic status, and authoritarian rather than liberal administration. These differences are conducive to higher levels of obedience for authority

Table 5.3: Mean of Authoritarianism by Sex, University, Major, and Parents'
Place of Residence

		Category	N	Mean
Variable	Sex	1 Male	624	1.23
		2 Female	906	1.03
	University	1 Lebanese	903	1.18
		2 American	627	1.01
	Major	1 Engineering & Agriculture	179	1.18
		2 Medicine & Health Sciences	148	0.88
		3 Basic Sciences	312	1.22
		4 Humanities & Social Sciences	891	1.10
	Parents' Education	0 Abroad	93	1.25
		1 Beirut City	466	1.07
		2 Suburbs of Beirut	321	1.09
		3 Other Mt. Lebanon	316	1.16
		4 Saida	47	1.02
		5 Other South Lebanon	90	1.09
		6 Tripoli	47	1.00
		7 Other North Lebanon	66	1.03
		8 Zahle or Baalback	54	1.37
		9 Other Beqa'	30	1.17

Grand Mean=1.11

among LU students than AUB students. Furthermore, the nature of the
student's major influences the intensity of his/her authoritarian attitudes.
Students majoring in basic sciences or engineering score higher on
authoritarianism than those in the humanities and social sciences. The
lowest scores on authoritarianism were found among students in the
medical and health sciences (table 5.3). Future physicians are socialized
to believe that they are indispensable to the public in their "sacred"

humanitarian profession and are given unique legal privileges and a high social status. Perhaps it is these facts that have permitted them to be less respectful of other authorities as compared with students majoring in the social sciences or engineering. Unlike engineers whose job places them under the mercy of capitalists and political rulers, doctors can work rather freely in any setting under any political or social authority.

The parents' place of residence also bears a significant relationship to authoritarian values. Most students approving of obedience to authority are those whose parents live in the cities of Zahleh and Baalback in the *muhafaza* of the Beqa' in East Lebanon. Least approving of the respect for, and obedience to, authority are students from the city of Tripoli, followed by the cities of Saida and Beirut, respectively (table 5.3). Perhaps the years of war, during which residents of the Beqa' were always under some form of political authority, have engendered in these students a stronger propensity toward the obedience of authority. By contrast, residents of the major coastal cities lived through several years of chaos where no single political authority was responsible for enforcing law and order.

Equalitarianism

Equalitarianism is an individual value characterized by "belief in the equality of all people, especially in political, economic, or social life."[18] To detect such a belief, students were asked whether they agree or disagree with the statement: "In a small group, there should be no real leaders—everyone should have an equal say."[19]

The overwhelming majority of AUB and LU students (80%) endorsed that statement (table 5.2). Equalitarianism is significantly related to sex, university, and mother's education (table 5.4). As expected, egalitarian beliefs are stronger among women than men, for women are the party struggling for gender equality (table A3). After centuries of subordination, Lebanese women are creating a power shift in gender relations through their egalitarian outlook and behavior.

LU students are more attached to egalitarian values than AUB students regardless of sex, social class, parents' educational level, or extent of religiosity (table A3). One possible explanation for this finding is the difference in admissions policy between the two universities. LU is much more lenient in admitting students than AUB, a policy that might have developed in its students' stronger feelings and beliefs in equality.

Table 5.4: Percentage of Students with Equalitarian Value by University, Sex, and Mother's Education.

Variable	% Students	Number of Students	X^2	DF	Significance of X^2
University					
Lebanese	88	1008			
American	68	641	92.89	1	<.0000
Sex					
Male	71	683			
Female	86	954	56.05	1	<.0000
Mother's Education					
Below Secondary	87	672			
Secondary	78	558			
University	72	397	42.13	2	<.0000

Another likely factor is the role of radical political parties. Since these parties promote equalitarianism and are more active among LU than AUB students, LU students may become more prone to these beliefs.

Strength of belief in equalitarianism varies negatively with mother's educational level. Children of highly educated women are less enthusiastic about equality among people than children of poorly educated women. There might be a social class dimension to this finding. Better-educated mothers do not feel equal to less educated counterparts, an attitude that may have been transmitted to their children.

Internal Control

The internal control index measures the extent to which an individual is in control of his/her life and actions. It is represented by a four-point index drawn from the following four statements with which the student can agree or disagree:

- My life is usually determined by my own actions.

- When I make plans, I am almost certain to make them work.
- I can pretty much determine what will happen in my life.
- When I get what I want, it is usually because I worked hard for it.[20]

The majority of respondents scored high on the index of individualism: a mean of 2.5 out of 4 and a median of 3.0 (table 5.1). A quarter scored the highest value of 4. That is students are generally in firm control of their lives and actions despite the long period of civil strife through which they passed.

There are two significant predictors of internal control: university and father's occupation, which acts as a proxy for social class (table 5.5). LU students have a stronger sense of control on their lives than AUB students (table 5.5). This contention may be due, at least in part, to the proclivity of LU students toward independence of mind and action because of the nature of the academic setting and their social class background. Middle class students (whose fathers are professionals) show the highest degree of internal control while upper class students (whose fathers are big business owners or managers) show the lowest control (table 5.5). Is it that professionals provide their children with a role model of self-reliance and high achievement on personal merit while business owners provide a role model of achievement based on social connections and good luck?

Fatalism

Fatalism or chance control is the degree of belief in chance factors or luck as determinants of one's life and actions. Using Arabic proverbs or expressions that denote fatalism, Western scholars describe the Arabs as fatalists without taking into account the "functions [the value of fatalism] served in particular circumstances."[21] Fatalism is measured here by a four-point index based on the following four statements with which the respondent can either agree or disagree:

- I have found that what is going to happen will happen.
- It's not always wise for me to plan too far ahead because many things turn out to be a matter of good or bad fortune.
- When I get what I want, it's usually because I'm lucky.
- To a great extent, my life is controlled by accidental happenings.[22]

Table 5.5: Mean of Internal Control Scale by University and Father's Occupation

		Category	N	Mean
Variable	University	1. Lebanese	764	2.88
		2. American	583	2.65
	Father's Occupation	1. Business Owner/Manager	474	2.74
		2. Professional	244	2.89
		3. Employee & Worker	629	2.78

Grand Mean=2.78

After fifteen years of political instability and the lack of law and order that made many aspects of life uncertain, one should expect the Lebanese to be fatalistic. In wartime, armed militias determined the nature of life in Lebanese society, sometimes deciding who lives and who dies. No one was certain they would make it to the next day since accidental happenings could occur at anytime—on the street, at home, in the office, or even while shopping or praying.

Nevertheless, half the respondents scored below 2.0 on the four-point index of fatalism (table 5.1), signifying a lack of adherence to fatalism by a substantial proportion. Fatalism bears a significant statistical relation with four personal attributes: sex, father's occupation, major, and university (table 5.6). Of these attributes, university is by far the strongest predictor of fatalism followed by sex.[23] LU students are much more fatalistic than AUB students. Several factors may explain this divergence, notably, religiosity, social class, and war experience. On average, LU students are more religious and belong to lower social classes than AUB students. LU students are also likely to have suffered from the war more than AUB students because of their lower class background. Wealthier people were able to shield their children from much of the adverse psychological effects of the war by relocating them to safer places in Lebanon or abroad.

Since both Islam and Christianity highlight the notion of fate, religious people are expected to believe more strongly in fate than the non-religious. The more important religion is in one's life, the more fatalistic he/she becomes (table 5.6). Lower class affiliation seems to be more conducive to fatalism than that of the upper and middle classes (table 5.6). Is it that the uncertainties of life in wartime for the underprivileged classes have engendered or reinforced fatalistic beliefs? Or could it be that the socially immobile, who are stuck in the lower rungs of the social stratification ladder, give up hope of radical improvement in their lives thus believing in fortune rather than rational planning? In a similar vein, some sociologists talked about the "culture of poverty" present in some societies. Adherents to this culture have no plans to change their status because they believe they are doomed to it.

The results illustrate that women tend to be more fatalistic than men are (table 5.6). This could be attributed in part to their higher level of religiosity. As for the effect of academic major on fatalism, students in professional schools—medicine and engineering—are least fatalistic while those in the humanities and social sciences are most fatalistic. Apparently, the nature of the curriculum and academic training that students undertake in professional schools teaches them to value the notions of planning and rational thinking more than those in the arts majors.[24]

Value Stereotypes

Noted scholars in the West have advocated that Arab culture is characterized by a host of value orientations, such as tribal solidarity (*asabiya*). *Asabiya* is measured by a dichotomous variable based on the statement, "I'll always side with my brother against my cousin and with my cousin against a non-relative." This sentence is a famous ancient proverb that dates back to pre-Islamic Arabia; it connotes the primacy of solidarity among close kin.

Face saving value indicates the degree of approval for observing face saving in social interactions. It is a three-point index that sums up "agree or disagree" answers to the following statements:

Table 5.6: Mean of Fatalism by Father's Occupation, Sex, University, and Major

Variable		Category	N	Mean
	Father's Occupation	1. Business & Professional	700	1.81
		2. Employees & Worker	602	2.11
	Sex	1. Male	512	1.67
		2. Female	790	2.16
	University	1. Lebanese	729	2.19
		2. American	573	1.62
	Major	1. Engineering & Agriculture	163	1.69
		2. Medicine & Health Sciences	122	1.71
		3. Basic Sciences	243	1.98
		4. Humanities & Social Sciences	774	2.04
	Religiosity	1. Religion Not Important At All	82	1.63
		2. Not Important	81	1.61
		3. Neutral	51	1.79
		4. Important	229	1.89
		5. Very Important	417	2.15

- One must preserve appearances when in the company of others, whether friends or enemies.
- One must not hide one's troubles and problems from friends.
- It's all right to lie in order to save one's face.[25]

The extent of dislike for team work is measured as an index by summing up the positive-negative responses to the following two questions:

- I'd rather have a room to myself than a shared house.
- I usually prefer to work alone than be part of a team.[26]

The extent of dislike for manual work is a three-point index composed of the following statements:

- I like to work with my hands.
- I never fix things that break down even when I know how to fix them. I always ask someone to do that.
- Manual work is inferior to mental work even if it pays better.[27]

Emphasis on form rather than content refers to the strength of the observance of form, style, or word at the expense of content, substance, or meaning. It is measured as a two-point index from the statements:

- When talking to people in Lebanon, one should pay attention to the style of the expressions more than their content.
- People in Lebanon are less moved by what you say than by how you say it.[28]

Emphasis on shame versus guilt indicates the strength of feelings of shame as opposed to guilt. Patai, the Western writer on Arab culture and society, described Arab society as "shame society." This value orientation is measured as a three-point index from the following statements:

- I always think of what people will say about my actions and behavior.
- I don't feel guilty if I do something wrong without being noticed

by anyone.
- Before I act on something, I always ask myself: What will people say?[29]

The majority of students did not conform to the descriptions offered by Western writers (table 5.1). They neither endorsed kinship solidarity unconditionally, nor shunned team work or disdain manual work, and nor did they display feelings of shame instead of guilt. Half of the students scored below the mid-point of the face saving variable. Only the responses to the form-content questions were different. A majority of the respondents considered the Lebanese society to prefer form to content, a finding that may not be applicable to other Arab societies. However, this value orientation in Lebanon fits one of the features of postmodern culture, namely its emphasis on "personal" image or style rather than character or occupation.

Students' responses vary by few background and personality attributes, notably, by university. LU students endorse the *asabiya* value more strongly than AUB students do (table A6). This is probably because there is a larger proportion of villagers among LU students. In rural Lebanon, tribal and kinship solidarity remains an important organizing force of social relations. They dislike manual work more than AUB students,[30] perhaps because many of them attribute their lower social status to the manual work of their fathers. Feelings of shame as opposed to guilt are stronger among LU than AUB students (table 5.7), as is the belief in the primacy of form over content (table 5.8). On the other hand, AUB students approve of the face-saving behavior more than LU students[31] do, and they also dislike team work more than LU students do (table A7). Again, the social background—rural/urban, poor/rich—may account for this difference by university.

Religious people tend to adopt kinship solidarity more than non-religious groups (table 5.9). To be sure, religion promotes family cohesion and solidarity, thus, religious people are expected to heed its message. Religion also encourages group work, as indicated in the relationship between dislike for team work and religiosity (table 26)

Gender is another significant correlate of social value stereotypes. Females have a stronger feeling of shame versus guilt than males (table 5.7); this can be related to the closer attention given by society to the appearance of girls than boys and to the various aspects of their social behavior. The modesty code remains relevant for a large

Table 5.7: Mean of Shame-Guilt Value by University and Sex

		Category	N	Mean
Variable	University	1. Lebanese	974	1.04
		2. American	634	0.92
	Sex	1. Male	665	1.08
		2. Female	943	0.93

Table 5.8: Mean of Form-Content Value by Sect, University and Sex

		Category	N	Mean
Variable	Sect	1. Maronite	288	0.60
		2. Catholic	100	0.48
		3. Orthodox	157	0.55
		4. Sunni	295	0.44
		5. Shiite	317	0.47
		6. Druze	128	0.44
	Sex	1. Male	496	0.45
		2. Female	789	0.53
	University	1. Lebanese	729	0.56
		2. American	556	0.41

proportion of the populace. In the same vein, one can understand why female students are more concerned about form than males (table 5.8).

Summary

Similar to Western students, Lebanese students scored high on the personal value of individualism and low on the value of authoritarianism. They espoused equalitarianism and showed a high level of internal control over their lives. The strongest determinants of most individual values were gender and university. As for societal values, the majority of students did not endorse kinship solidarity unconditionally, did not shun team work or disdain manual work, and had no feelings of shame instead of guilt.

CHAPTER 6

FAMILY NORMS: PERSISTENCE AND CHANGE

> The Lord hath decreed
> That ye worship none but Him,
> And that ye be kind
> To parents.
>
> The Holy Koran[1]

One's self is a set of different identities; it is multifaceted, with distinct identities organized in a hierarchical manner. These identities are "self-cognitions tied to roles, and through roles to positions in organized social relationships."[2] The relationships develop within specific social groups such as family and religious community. Through the process of socialization, which begins with birth and ends with death, an individual develops a set of reference groups with which he/she identifies. These groups provide normative guidance and role models for one's behavior; they are not equally important to all people, for some satisfy more needs than others on the psychological, social, economic, and legal levels. Hence, reference groups are thought to form a hierarchical order such that the higher in rank is more durable and persistent than the lower.[3]

This chapter examines the set of social groups that the Lebanese students identify with and points out their hierarchical order. It also investigates the effect of predetermined background variables, such as gender, social class, religion, and political ideology, on students' group affiliations. Since there is wide agreement among scholars that the family is the basic social institution in Arab societies, including the Lebanese, it is studied here at some length. Analyzed are relations within the family, which have evolved over time, especially between students and their parents, the nature of their disputes, and how they resolve them. A general pattern of relations within the family is described as well as variations of that pattern by gender, major, social class, level of education of parents, religious affiliation, and degree of religiosity.

Comparable data on group affiliations of Arab students at AUB date back to 1957-58 and 1970-71.[4] Since these baseline data refer to a diversity of Arab nationalities that employed a different instrument than the one used in this study, the comparison is not methodologically flawless. However, the common features of the social structure in Arab countries make this comparison reasonable. Moreover, it is the only available data from the pre-war period. Another comparable data set from pre-war Lebanon is from Barakat's study, *Civil Strife in Lebanon*. His data deal with family relations and issues among AUB students, more than half of whom are Lebanese. The current data set is from two surveys of AUB students and one from LU students. The AUB data were collected in the spring of 1993 and in the spring of 1996 and the LU data in the fall of 1996.

Group Affiliations

Despite their importance to the Lebanese, confessional loyalties do not supersede family and parochial ties. Yet, all of these primordial allegiances in modern Lebanon are part of what Hisham Sharabi terms "neo-patriarchy."[5] As explained in chapter 4, neo-patriarchy refers to a new form of patriarchy that pervades Arab society; it is neither modern, nor traditional, but possesses the basic non-egalitarian features of patriarchy. The building block of the neo-patriarchal society is the family.

Melikian and Diab's surveys of Arab college students in 1957 and 1970 showed a persistent pattern of group affiliations over time: the family was the most important identity group followed by the ethnic/national group. Religion ranked third in importance in the 1957 survey but citizenship occupied that rank in the 1970 survey.[6] These surveys, however, did not distinguish between the nuclear family (*usrah*), the extended family (*'ailah*), and the clan or tribe.

In the surveys used in this study, a distinction was made between nuclear and extended families. The rationale is that the Arab and Lebanese extended family is a typical patriarchal family, while the

Table 6.1: Group Affiliations of Lebanese Students by University, 1996

Social Group	Closest Group (%)		Second Closest Group (%)		Third Closest Group (%)	
	AUB	LU	AUB	LU	AUB	LU
Nuclear Family	63	49				
Extended Family			28	29		
Geographic Area of Residence or Birth					38	46
Number of Students	**640**	**999**	**638**	**954**	**624**	**903**

Table 6.2: Group Affiliations of Lebanese Students at AUB by Year

Social Group	Closest Group (%)		Second Closest Group (%)		Third Closest Group (%)	
	1993	1996	1993	1996	1993	1996
Nuclear Family	61	63				
Extended Family			33	28		
Geographic Area of Residence or Birth					43	38
Number of Students	**794**	**640**	**787**	**638**	**757**	**624**

nuclear family is a modern form that embodies different norms and social relations. Authoritarianism of the father and dependency of all other members characterize the relations among members of a typical patriarchal family. A Lebanese psychologist described the pattern of socialization of the child in a traditional Lebanese family in the following terms:

> The family is relentless in its repression. [The child] is brought up to become an obedient youth, subservient to those above him—his father, older brother, clan chief, president.[7]

By contrast, the nuclear western family shows significant egalitarianism and democratic relations among its members.

At AUB, from 1993 to 1996, and at LU in 1996, Lebanese students overwhelmingly considered their nuclear families the closest social group with which they identify irrespective of their sex, social class, religion, or extent of religiosity. Next in importance was the extended family, followed by the place of birth or residence, and religion (tables 6.1 and 6.2). Not only are these findings safely generalized to all college students but to all Lebanese adults as well. The very high level of statistical significance, along with the consistency of the findings over time in the data collected for this study and those of Melikian and Diab, offer ample assurance of their reliability. Hence, the claim that some authors make regarding the priority of confession over the family is empirically false.[8] The data show that a Lebanese person is first a member of a given family from a specific region with a particular religious affiliation before he is a Lebanese.

One interesting new finding retrieved from the data is the continuous rise in the percentage of AUB students identifying with their peer group. The percentage choosing their friends as the second closest group increased from 13% in 1993 to 17% in 1996, with no significant difference by sex. Peer group appears to be replacing the extended family, place of residence/birth, and religion as a reference group for many middle and upper class youth.

A noteworthy differential in group identification is by gender. Female students at both AUB and LU in all three surveys identified with their nuclear families as their closest social group more strongly than male students did. This gender difference is statistically significant at the 0.0001 level (tables 6.3 and 6.4). At LU, there is also a significant gender difference in group identification for the second and third closest group

Table 6.3: Three Closest Groups to AUB Students by Sex and Year

Social Group	1993					1996				
	Male (%)	Female (%)	X^2	DF	Sig. of X^2	Male (%)	Female (%)	X^2	DF	Sig of X^2
Nuclear Family, Closest Group	53	71	26.9	1	<.0001	54	72	22.9	1	<.0001
Extended Family, 2nd Closest Group	30	36	3.2	1	>.05	24	31	3.7	1	>.05
Geographic Area of Residence or Birth, 3rd Closest Group	44	36	4.3	1	>.05	34	41	3.2	1	>.05
Number of Students	454	341				299	340			

Table 6.4: The Three Closest Groups to LU Students by Sex, 1996

Social group	Male (%)	Female (%)	X^2	DF	Sig. of X^2
Nuclear Family , Closest Group	38%	55%	26.9	1	<.0001
Extended Family, 2nd Closest Group	23%	30%	6.8	1	<.01
Geographic Area of Residence or Birth, 3rd Closest Group	36%	47%	11.4	1	<.01
Number of Students	**86**	**617**			

(table 6.4).

By expressing distinctive attachment to their immediate families, college girls probably reflect a continuous sense of dependency on their families. Prevalent social norms, practices, and Lebanese laws are not very supportive of the new modern roles assumed by women in Western societies. The image of the assertive, independent, and outspoken woman is not yet totally welcome. Under such circumstances, it is not surprising that female students cling tightly to their nuclear families, which act as safety nets for them to fall back on if and when society lets them down. By the same token, their stronger adherence to other parochial entities— extended family and the local community—in comparison with men, testifies to their strong sense of insecurity concerning their human rights, welfare, and status in the larger Lebanese society. For women, life outside the contours of the family, clan, and local community is particularly replete with uncertainty, gender stereotypes, and injustice.

In the 1993 AUB survey, a question on political orientation was asked. Results of the data analysis show a significant association between political ideology and group affiliation. The proportion of students who identified the nuclear family as the closest group was highest among Lebanese nationalists, followed by Arab nationalists and then Islamists (table 6.5). For example, 64% of the Lebanese nationalists

Table 6.5: The Three Closest Groups to AUB Students by Political Orientation, 1993

Social Group	Lebanese Nationalism (%)	Arab Nationalism (%)	Islamsim (%)	X^2	DF	Sig. of X^2
Nuclear Family, Closest Group	64	58	45	8.4	2	<.05
Extended Family, 2nd Closest Group	34	36	18	7.5	2	<.05
Geographic Area of Residence or Birth, 3rd Closest Group	44	34	28	8.5	2	<.05
Number of Students	**538**	**127**	**60**			

Table 6.6: Percentage of AUB Students Who Agree with Each of the Following Statements on Kinship Ties, 1993*

Question	% Agree or Yes
I am strongly attached to my family	92
Consider oneself most closely tied to one's family (parents and siblings)	63
Ties with extended family members are very close and intimate with frequent visits and mutual assistance	35
Ties with extended family member are somewhat close with occasional visits and mutual assistance	55

* Number of students is 793

singled out their immediate families as the closest group, as compared to 58% of Arab nationalists and 45% of the Islamists. The same pattern of difference by political ideology was observed among students who selected the place of residence or birth as their third closest group. In selecting the extended family as the second closest group, Lebanese and Arab nationalists were similar to each other.

The nuclear family was the most important social group regardless of one's political ideology. However, in comparison with the Lebanese and Arab nationalists, fewer Islamists were close to the three most important reference groups. Furthermore, it must be remarked that they were the only category of students that considered religious sect to be the second closest identity group. This comes as no surprise since their political ideology requires identification with one's religious community. At LU, although no question on political ideology was asked, one can get a rough idea about the ranking of religious sect among Islamists. This was done by examining the hierarchy of groups among the Shiites who selected a Hizbullah political representative or spiritual guide as their most liked leader. For this category of students, sect and extended family tied for the second place in the order of reference groups (27% versus 28%), a finding close to that of AUB.

Over 90% of AUB students in 1993 reported strong or very strong bonds that link them to their families (table 6.6). These bonds vary significantly by religiosity and political ideology. Believers in God who practiced religious rituals on a regular or occasional basis were most closely attached to their families. Students who did not practice rites and those who did not believe in God expressed weaker attachment to their families (table 6.7). As to political ideology, all Islamists without exception (100%) reported strong or very strong family bonds as compared to 92% and 93% of Arab nationalists and Lebanese nationalists, respectively (table 6.7).

Relations within the Family

AUB students' overall relation with their parents remains as close as it was in 1970. However, certain aspects of this relation have changed. AUB students are now more attached to their mothers than they were before the war (tables 6.8 and 6.9). Since the mother is not the symbol of authority and dominance in traditional Arab society, this finding may reflect a weakening in the authority of the father, the patriarch, within the

Table 6.7: Percentage of AUB Students Who are Strongly Attached to their Families by Religiosity and Political Orientation, 1993

	% Attached	Number of Students	X^2	DF	Sig. of X^2
Political Orientation:			8.4	2	<.05
Lebanese Nationalism	93	535			
Arab Nationalism	92	127			
Islamism	100	60			
Religiosity			26.5	3	<.0001
Believer and Regualr Practice of Rites	96	244			
Believer and Occasional Practice of Rites	97	168			
Believer and No Practice of Rites	88	294			
Nonbeliever	82	62			

Table 6.8: Relation of AUB Students to Their Parents, 1970 and 1994

	CLOSENESS TO:		
	BOTH PARENTS	EACH OF THE PARENTS	
EXTENT OF CLOSENESS	1970* (%)	1994 (%)	
		FATHER	MOTHER
Very close	43	26	48
On good terms, 1970 (close/somewhat close, 1994)	44	60	47
Not close/don't get along well	9	8	4
Total %	**100**	**100**	**100**

*Source: Barakat, 1977, Appendix, p. 205.

Table 6.9: AUB Students' Preference for Any of the Two Parents, 1970 and 1994

STUDENTS' PREFERENCE	1970* (%)	1994 (%)
Closer to father (1970)/ Get along better with father (1994)	11	12
Closer to mother (1970)/ Get along better with mother (1994)	30	48
Equally close to both (1970)/ Get along well with both (1994)	50	36
Neither (1970)/ Don't get along with any (1994)	5	2
Total %	**100**	**100**
Number of Students	**213**	**477**

*Source: Barakat, 1977, Appendix, p. 205

family. It may also indicate a tendency toward democratic practices in the family. Other more direct signs corroborate this inference, as elaborated later when discussing changes in the authority structure of the family.

Issues of Dispute and Their Resolution

Relations between parents and their young adult children are characterized by constant disputes. Issues of dispute range from trivial things like eating and sleeping habits, social etiquette (such as dress codes), and socializing with peers, to more serious decisions such as career choice and selection of mates. Frequently, parent-children disputes stem from unfulfilled expectations or aspirations of either party.

The data show that the major issues of dispute between AUB students and their parents involve the mode of interaction with parents, social behavior, and academic performance. Students upset their parents when they engage in certain activities or behave in "unacceptable" ways. By the same token, parents upset the students when their behavior does not conform to the children's expectations. The parents of more than half the students were most upset for being yelled back at and ignored deliberately. Most students, on the other hand, were outraged when their parents lied to them or treated them like small children (table 6.10). Such issues of dispute are not unique to Lebanese youth. They are common in any parent-child relationship. The general explanation for their prevalence stems from the social and psychological characteristics of development that a child goes through and the slow process of adjustment that parents undergo when their children reach adolescence then adulthood.

Talking back to one's parents and ignoring them are viewed as a violation of the norm of respect for elders as well as parents, a norm that is widely held in various societies. On the other hand, parents also violate social norms when they lie to their children. Therefore, by resenting parents' lies, students uphold the moral norm they were raised to adopt—namely, that role models like parents should be virtuous, honest, and candid. Furthermore, the students' anger at being treated like children stems from their recently acquired belief that they are grown-ups and should be treated as such. The parents, however, cannot easily forgo perceiving the students as the little children they have reared for years.

Table 6.10: Percentage of AUB Students Who Experienced Each of the Following Issues of Dispute With Their Parents, 1994

Question*	% Agree**
My parents get upset when I yell back at them.	65
My parents get upset when I intentionally ignore them (both or either).	55
I get upset when my parents treat me like a child.	54
I get upset when my parents don't tell me the truth.	53
Number of Students	**444**

* The exact question wording was as follows:
In each of the statements below, specify how often that thing happens to you. Does it happen: (5) always (4) often (2) seldom or (1) never. The percentages reported refer to the combined answers "always" and "often."
**All percentages reported exceed 50%. Issues reported by fewer students are not included.

Table 6.11: Percentage of Male and Female AUB Students Who Experienced Each of the Following Issues of Dispute With Their Parents, 1994

Question	% Agree* Male	Female
My parents get upset when I yell back at them.	59	72
My parents get upset when I don't tell them where I am going.	42	56
My parents get upset when I stay out later than I am allowed to.	26	50
Number of Students	**250**	**194**

*All sex differences in the percentages reported are statistically significant the 0.01 level.

Girls outrage parents more than boys do when they respond to their parents in a loud voice (table 6.11). In prevalent traditional norms, a woman follows a modesty code, which requires that women speak softly to others, especially to those in positions of family authority, notably, the parents, husband, and the elderly male kin. Less irritating is the boys' violation of this norm, although it is by no means unimportant since about 60% of the parents were irritated by their sons when they shouted back. In both Christianity and Islam, respect for parents is highly stressed. In the Koran, the parents' reverence is an obligation to all Muslims, men and women alike. The Koranic verse pertaining to this injunction is very strong in unequivocal terms, placing parents' respect in importance right after God's worship, which is the first and foremost criterion for being a Muslim:

> The Lord hath decreed
> That ye worship none but Him,
> And that ye be kind
> To parents. Whether one
> Or both of them attain
> Old age in thy life,
> Say not to them a word
> Of contempt, nor repel them,
> But address them
> In terms of honor.
> And out of kindess
> Lower to them the wing
> Of humility, and say:
> "My Lord! Bestow on them
> Thy Mercy even as they
> Cherished me in childhood."[9]

Two other issues of dispute relate to the students' social behavior even though they were reported by fewer than half of the students—namely, not reporting their whereabouts to their parents and staying out past curfew. Slightly less than half of the students' parents were angered when their children kept them in the dark about their whereabouts, and 37% were upset when their children stayed out late exceeding their curfew time. Although they are less prevalent than being yelled at, the two issues show appreciable correlation with gender (table 6.11), and one issue—staying out late—was singled out by students as the most important issue of conflict with their parents (table 6.12).

Table 6.12: The Three Most Important Issues of Dispute Between AUB Students and Their Parents, As Perceived by Students, by Sex of Student, 1994

Degree of Importance	Issue of Dispute	Male (%)	Female (%)
Most important	Staying out late at night	13	25
Second most important	College work	16	9
Third most important	Social and religious values	9	18
Number of Students		**233**	**174**

Parents in patriarchal, cohesive families that prevail in the Arab Levant are typically overprotective of their children, who reside with them even when they reach the legal age of twenty-one. Most students, males and females alike, agreed that their parents were overprotective. In wartime Lebanon, this overprotection took a different dimension reaching a state of phobia. People's experience in the war has created excessive feelings of anxiety and fear about their loved ones. These feelings were born at a time when the movement of any person from one place to another, regardless of distance, was often wrought with the risk of kidnapping, injury, or death. At that time, the state and its agencies were in total disarray, and people had to rely on their own resources to protect their loved ones. In the event of a tragic incident, for example, parents could immediately intervene to help out in more ways than one using their own social network and connections. Therefore, keeping track of the whereabouts of their "significant others," especially their children, was only a rational, cautionary measure for people, and also the only one available.

The concern of parents over the safety of the students is manifested in the disputes they engage in over staying out late and not informing them where they are. Female children pose an additional source of worry for parents since the modesty, or honor code, for women (notion of *'ird*) still prevails in Lebanese society. In a survey of Lebanese adult women conducted in 1995 by this author, the overwhelming majority of ever-married women (73%), regardless of religious persuasion, wished to see their daughters safeguard their virginity until marriage. Twice as many parents of AUB female students as male students (50% versus 26%) were upset to see their children stay out late at night.

Besides gender, religious affiliation influences parents' tolerance of children's late outings. Christian parents of various persuasions were more approving of students' outings than Muslim parents were. Historically, many Lebanese Christians identified more with Western social values and behavior that encourage the independence of children at an earlier age than did Muslims. Among Muslims, the Shiites were most tolerant (table 6.13). The distinction of the Shiite position cannot be attributed to religiosity, father's educational attainment, or mother's education because the data did not support such hypotheses. Perhaps the propensity of Shiism as a doctrine to encourage unorthodox opinions in religion through rational rulings (*ijtihad*) could account for this result.

The most common method that students employed to resolve disputes with their parents was to confront and discuss the problem with them, irrespective of the gravity of the dispute (table 6.14). Most students adopted this approach regardless of their religion, sex, social class, or educational level of their parents. This indicates a transition in the nature of relations between parents and their adult children, which were once governed by absolute authority of the father and total obedience of children irrespective of their age. By initiating a discussion of the disputing issues with the parents, students are asserting their independent identity as well as determination to maintain cohesive family bonds. Likewise, the parents' willingness to listen to their children explain their position in the conflict signifies a decline in authoritarianism and patriarchy in the family.

A small minority of students (13% and 12%) reported resorting to two other methods. One method was that students ignored the conflict completely as if nothing happened while maintaining normal relations with their parents. Another was the parents' tendency to discuss the problem and explain their point of view to their children.

Nucleation and Democratization of the Family

The extended family, which predominated in Lebanon for generations, has been on the decline for some time, reaching 22% in 1996.[10] Behind this decline is a mixture of factors, notably, the economy and the civil war. The capitalist economy, by its nature, leads to the loosening of social bonds within clans and extended families, as the

Table 6.13: Percentage of Parents Upset with AUB Students Over Staying Out Late by Religion, 1994

	Maronite & Catholic	Orthodox	Sunni	Shiite	Druze	X^2	DF	Sig. of X^2
Parents Upset Over Staying Out Late	27	25	49	32	42	19.3	4	<.01
Number of Students	**93**	**75**	**148**	**78**	**38**			

Table 6.14: The Three Most Important Methods of Conflict Resolution

Degree of Importance	Method of Conflict Resolution	Male (%)	Female (%)
Most Important	Student Discusses Problem With Parents	56	64
Second Most Important	Student Ignores the Conflict and Continues to Interact with Parents as Usual	18	8
Third Most Important	Parents Try to Discuss the Problem With Student, Giving Him/Her their Point of View	10	13
Number of Students		**248**	**192**

historical experience of Western countries demonstrates.   Lebanon's capitalist economy and its integration into that of the world are expected to reinforce this outcome. As to social change, the impact of education, together with technological transfer and exposure to Western values through international mass media, present a new model for the family that many have emulated.   Moreover, civil war nurtured tight social ties among people living in the same building or locality, irrespective of their kinship relation; they had to spend days together in the same shelter, sharing food and comforting each other. As a result, members of the extended family who did not live in physical proximity drew farther apart, thereby weakening their pre-war tight bonds.

Besides children forming tighter bonds with their mothers—an indirect sign of democratization of the Lebanese family—the data include three direct, strong indicators of democratization. One relates to the level of the mother's participation in decision-making, another to the students' adherence to gender equality, and the last indicator concerns the students' personal values of authoritarianism and individualism.

The first indicator shows an increasing participation of mothers in making decisions about significant issues relating to their family. In 1994, AUB students were asked to specify the primary decision-maker in their families on each of the following matters:

- Selection of food for the family's meals
- Selection of the family physician
- Selection of the family lawyer
- Selection of the family bank, and which schools children go to
- Whether or not to buy a car/furniture/land, and details of the purchase (such as the car make)
- Type of house the family would live in (number of rooms, location, ...)
- Which person the student may marry

While mothers remain the predominant decision-maker with regard to food selection and cooking (71% of the cases), they now make joint decisions with their husbands on almost all other issues. The only major exception being the choice of the bank, which the father usually decides. All grown-up members of the nuclear family participate on certain matters, like the type of house and neighborhood the family plans to move to. As for the selection of the prospective spouse for the students, the students themselves are primarily the decision-makers.

The level of the mother's educational attainment is, to a great extent, the best predictor of her participation in the decision making of the family. A considerably higher level of participation was reported for college educated mothers as opposed to those who did not complete secondary education (table 6.15). The education difference in participation rates was impressive, depending on the issue under consideration. For example, this difference by education was 22% in the case of selecting a lawyer and 32% when selecting a school for the children. Therefore, it is no longer accurate to state that relations within the Lebanese nuclear family are patriarchal. This change is commensurate with a loosening of ties between the nuclear and the extended family. While attachment to the nuclear family is reported by the vast majority of AUB students to be very strong (92%), the relations with their relatives in the extended family are only somewhat close with occasional visits (55%) (table 6.5).

Another indicator of democratization is the strength of the gender equality norm among college students. Wide acceptance and support for gender equality is reflected in the students' answers to a set of questions that measure gender stereotypes (table 6.16). The overwhelming majority of both male and female students at AUB had no preference for working under a male boss, and the sex of the work supervisor was not an important issue to them. All believed that women are not "inferior to men" and "should be allowed to work outside the home irrespective of their marital status (i.e., being single, married, divorced, or widowed)." Wives, the students asserted, "should have an equal say to their husbands in all family matters" and should gain access to the husbands' bank accounts as well. Most women disapproved of the traditional social norm that considers "the most important role for a woman...to be a housewife-mother." In contrast, only half the men held that opinion (table 6.16).

While no relevant pre-war data on traditional social norms are available for comparison, all the scholarly work on the Lebanese family before 1975 points to its prevalence. Hence, the data presented portray a strong, genuine, normative change in the direction of gender equality. This change in gender equality reflects a wider, more encompassing societal transformation that has reached various segments of the population. In the 1995 survey of adult women conducted by this author, a similar set of questions was asked about the decision making process within families. The findings were quite consistent with those of AUB

Table 6.15: Percentage of Families of AUB Students in Which the Mother Decides Alone or Jointly With the Father on Selected Matters by Mother's Level of Education, 1994

Mother's Education	**Family Matter**					No. of Mothers
	Selection Of: Physician	Lawyer	Kids' School	House	Land	
Less than Secondary	35	35	56	34	28	91
College & Higher	59	57	88	57	53	129

students.[11] The majority of Lebanese wives reported playing a major role in the important family decisions, a clear break with traditional family practices.

Still, the majority of students—more males than females—did not adopt all the ideas and norms that govern gender equality in Western societies. For example, most AUB students did not accept the notions that women can take on any job, or that premarital sex for girls should be tolerated. Also, almost half the students opposed allowing mothers with young children to work outside their homes, for they believed that mothers should give priority to childrearing (table 6.16).

To investigate the correlates of gender stereotypes further—as portrayed by AUB students—an index of sexism composed of all the indicators in table 6.16 was constructed. Stereotypes are defined as well learned, widely shared, socially validated, general beliefs about women.[12] The index ranges from a lowest level of 0 to a highest level of 10 since 10 dichotomous indicators were summed up, each assuming one of two scores 0 or 1. The low level of the index signifies a student's approval of gender equality and adoption of modern attitudes toward women, while a high level implies the disapproval of gender equality and adherence to traditional norms toward women

The average score of the female stereotype index was 4.4, mid-way between the extreme low and high values. Half the students scored

Table 6.16: Percentage of Male and Female AUB Students Who Agree With
Each of the Following Statements on Family and Gender Issues, 1994

Question	% Agree Male	% Agree Female
A housewife should have access to her husband's bank account either by having a joint account or a separate account for herself.	84	92
Wives should have an equal say to their husbands in all family matters.	81	90
I prefer to work under a male boss.	36	33
Women should be allowed to work outside the home irrespective of their marital status (i.e., being single, married, divorced, or widowed).	86	90
Mothers with young children should not be allowed to work outside the home.	49	44
Some jobs are inappropriate for women.	80	60
The most important social role for a woman is to be a housewife-mother.	50	40
Women are inferior to men.	17	6
Premarital sex in our society should be allowed for both boys and girls.	53	33
A girl should remain a virgin until marriage.*	54	67
My father is very authoritarian and domineering.	24	28
Number of Students	**250**	**194**

* al-Amin and Faour found that 38% of males and 64% of females in 1997 did not agree with the statement, "When a girl loses her virginity, she brings shame on herself and her family."

below 4.0 (median=4.0) and half the students scored a 4.0 and above, which implies a weak tendency toward lower levels of stereotypic beliefs. Four factors altogether explain a good deal of the variation (18.5%) in these beliefs: sex, social class, religiosity, and sect (table A9). Each is significantly related to the index (tables 6.17 and A8). Women tended to hold less stereotypic views about themselves than men did, possibly as a result of their higher education. Since one of the explicit objectives of university education is to enhance the self-esteem of students, it is not surprising that this objective is much more relevant to females than males. After all, Lebanese and Arab women may have lower self-esteem than men as a result of the lack of gender equality in most Arab countries.[13]

Apparently, students are influenced by the sexist attitudes of their fathers. Other factors being equal, children of blue-collar workers were less favorable toward gender equality than those whose fathers were businessmen, professionals, or white-collar workers. Put differently, students from a lower class background had more stereotypic views of women than those from middle or upper class backgrounds. One can relate this difference to the general view held by most students that typical blue-collar jobs are only for men. Women, they claim, should not engage in work that requires physical strength; in Lebanon and other Arab countries, one rarely finds women in such occupations. Therefore, blue-collar men who are accustomed to working in an exclusively male setting are more likely to hold stereotypic beliefs about women. Conversely, men in other occupations are less likely to develop such beliefs.

Traditional views of women rise monotonically with the degree of religiosity. Indeed, net of all other factors, religiosity is the single most important predictor of gender stereotypes. Christians were found to be least stereotypic about women, followed by the Druze, while Muslims were most stereotypic, with the Shiites scoring the highest value. One can explain this difference in terms of the differential socialization of Christians and Muslims. The former are raised to see the West as a model society with its values and norms, while the latter are raised with the Islamic pristine society as the model. Evidently, the two models have widely disparate perceptions of gender and women's role in society. As to the difference between the Druze and mainstream Muslims, again this is a reflection of their differential upbringing. The Druze children are not socialized by their families as devout Muslims who look up to the pristine

Table 6.17: Mean Value of the Index of Strength of Female Stereotypes by Sex, Religiosity, Sect, and Social Class

		Category	N	Mean
Variable	Sex	1 Male	200	4.17
		2 Female	152	0.18
	Religiosity	0 Non-Believer	27	2.78
		1 Believer & No Practice	158	4.25
		2 Believer & Occasional Practice	62	4.74
		3 Believer & Regular Practice	105	5.10
	Sect	1 Maronite &Catholic	70	3.91
		2 Orthodox	62	3.97
		3 Sunni	122	4.84
		4 Shiite	66	5.00
		5 Druze	32	4.28
	Father's Occupation	1 Worker	92	4.79
		2 All Other Occupations	260	4.37

Islamic society as a model. An overwhelming majority of the Druze students either do not observe any religious rites (73%), or are nonbelievers in God (19%).

Finally, the third indicator of nucleation and democratization of the Lebanese family is the level of authoritarianism, individualism, and egalitarianism as individual values among AUB and LU students in 1996. Although the subject of individual values was discussed in the preceding chapter, the relevance of the aforementioned indicators to the question of the nucleation of the family calls for a brief exposition. Authoritarianism indicates the degree of obedience and respect for authority; individualism refers to the extent of independence from others and being the master of one's fate; and egalitarianism measures the strength of belief in equality within groups. More than one in every five students scored lowest on the authoritarian scale. The average score was also low, a sign of limited respect for authority. On the scale of individualism, more than one in every three students scored highest. The average score was high, showing a high level of individualism among the Lebanese youth. On egalitarianism, 80% of the students thought every one in a small group should have an equal say.[14]   Again, that testifies to a high level of egalitarian norms.

In addition to the three indicators mentioned above, an observation in support of the trend toward democratic relations within the Lebanese family may be of interest to the reader.   Recently, an unprecedented practice has been observed within the Muslim family, including this writer's own extended family: marriage contracts that empower the wife with the so-called 'isma (the woman's right to divorce her husband).   Traditionally, only husbands have the right to initiate divorce among Muslims. While Islamic law allows the wife to place in the marriage contract a clause that states her right to initiate divorce, the centuries-long predominance of patriarchal norms and practices have made its implementation very rare.[15]

Summary

Lebanese students identify most closely with their nuclear family, irrespective of other group affiliations, followed by their extended family, place of residence/birth, and religious sect, respectively. AUB students maintain close relations with their parents but occasionally engage in disputes with them, which they usually resolve through discussion. The main issues of dispute are the social behavior of the students and their academic performance. The data reveal signs of democratization of the Lebanese family—mainly, a high level of the mother's participation in decision-making concerning family matters and a strong adherence by students to gender equality.

CHAPTER 7

POLITICAL ATTITUDES AND NORMS

> They are killing it [freedom], yes because it is for the sake of the individual and it exists within him/her.
> And the human within them [alluding to political rulers] has died, and so has mercy. Death has created in them grudge, injustice, oppression, and greed.
> Woe on them from the people's wrath, from the roaring of lions when freed from their cages.
> Woe on those who do not have mercy on others while in power for they will not find any who will be merciful to them when the revolution erupts.
>
> Elissa El-Hashem[1]

In examining the attitudes and norms of Lebanese college students regarding a host of political issues, this chapter addresses the following questions: What are the opinions of these students concerning major political issues and problems that the nation is confronting? How different are the opinions of postwar students from those of their pre-war counterparts in that respect? What are some of the social and economic correlates of students' political norms? Do students' perceptions of political life accurately reflect political realities?

The postwar data are drawn from a random sample of Lebanese students at AUB in the spring of 1993 and a purposive sample of students at LU in the fall of 1996. Since the AUB data are based on a probability sample, the findings are generalized to the total Lebanese student population at AUB. The LU data, however, are not generalized to the total LU student population as the sample is a non-probability sample; the data are sensitive to the composition of the sample, particularly by religious sect. However, the LU data provide valid inference about all LU students belonging to each sect in the total LU student population.

As to the comparable pre-war data set, it is drawn mainly from Halim Barakat's study, *Lebanon in Strife*.[2]   Barakat's AUB sample, however, is composed of both Lebanese and non-Lebanese Arab students, while his LU sample includes Lebanese students only.   Since political orientations of students may vary by nationality, Barakat's AUB data on political orientations are not that comparable to the data in this study. Instead, it is more meaningful to compare the AUB data in this study with Barakat's LU data since both refer to Lebanese students only.

Two other pre-war surveys of students are utilized for partial comparison: the first by Hanf[3] and the second by Nasr and Palmer.[4] Relevant findings of a third survey conducted during the war by Khashan[5] will also be used, yet with caution given the different methodological and operational differences between Khashan's study and the present one.

This chapter also examines the variation of students' attitudes, perceptions, and norms by such background attributes as gender, religious affiliation, social class, university, and college major.

Political Leaders

Students' attitudes toward political leaders can be positive, negative, or neutral. Students show a positive disposition toward the politicians they favor most and a negative disposition towards those they dislike most. Those who display neutral attitudes have no strong feelings for any political leader. In Lebanon, students' attitudes toward political leaders are influenced by a host of factors: religious affiliation, political orientation, economic conditions in the country, important regional and international events that immediately precede the opinion poll, and relevant information received from the mass media.

When asked in late 1996 who is your most liked political leader,[6] 32% of LU students named a local Christian Maronite politician, 16% a Shiite, 14% an Orthodox, and 11% a Sunni (table 7.1). The exiled General Michel Aoun, a Maronite, was relatively most popular with 15% of students naming him as the most liked leader. The next most liked politician was the Orthodox pan-Arab opposition member of parliament Najah Wakim, who was singled out by 13% of the students. The third rank in popularity was a tie among the Sunni Premier Rafiq Hariri, leading figures of Hizbullah Muhammad Hussein Fadlallah and Hasan Nasrallah, and the late pan-Arab President of Egypt, Gamal Abdel-Nasser.[7]

In contrast, AUB students in 1993 had a different selection of preferred leaders. Over 16% of them named a local Sunni politician and 15% a Maronite. Leaders of other Arab countries and other non-Arab countries were most preferred by 11% and 10% of the students, respectively. Among the most favored local politicians, Hariri and Aoun tied for the first rank, each garnering the support of 11% of students. More importantly, historical towering figures like the Prophet Muhammad, Gamal Abdel-Nasser, and Ghandi were identified as the most preferred leaders by 30% of students (table 7.1).[8] In other words, a large percentage of AUB students could not find one politician eligible enough to be a model leader within their own nation or among current world leaders. A plausible explanation is that their wider exposure to the outside world, in comparison with LU students,[9] allowed them to look far beyond their national borders and way back into the past for a model politician. The AUB students tended to favor leaders among the historical, charismatic figures who left permanent marks on world history.

Most disliked by LU students in 1996 were local politicians. About 32% of students named a Sunni politician, 18% a Maronite, 17% an Orthodox, and 14% a regional leader (table 7.1). Of the regional leaders, Israeli politicians were most hated. Among the local politicians mentioned, Hariri was most disliked, garnering 29% of the students' votes, followed by 13% for the Minister of the Interior, the Orthodox Michel Murr.[10]

Conversely, AUB students in 1993 chose a different set of leaders to hate. Over 32% of them named a Maronite politician as the most disliked, 22% a regional leader, and 18% an international leader. Again, Israeli politicians topped the list of detested regional leaders. As for international leaders, most loathed were former President of the U.S.A., George Bush, and former head of the USSR, Vladimir Gorbachev (table 7.1). Of the local names most abhorred, the incarcerated head of the banned Lebanese Forces, Samir Ja'ja', was mentioned by 11% of the students, and Aoun by more than 7%.[11]

AUB students' dislike of Ja'ja', preference for Hariri, and the odd mixture of love and hate feelings toward Aoun illustrate the sensitivity of people's opinions to current events, particularly as portrayed by the mass

Table 7.1: Most Liked and Most Disliked Leaders by University (%)

CATEGORY OF LEADER	MOST LIKED		MOST DISLIKED	
	AUB, 1993	LU, 1996	AUB, 1993	LU, 1996
Sunni	16	11	3	32
Shiite	6	16	6	6
Druze	3	7	2	2
Maronite	15	32	33	18
Orthodox	0	14	0	17
Other local	4	1	1	1
Regional (Middle East)	11	4	22	14
International	10	3	18	2
Other: Historical, Nonpolitical	30	9	8	3
None	5	3	5	5
All politicians	0	0	2	0
Total	**100**	**100**	**100**	**100**
No. of Students	**751**	**801**	**740**	**736**

media. For example, Ja'ja' was most detested in the 1993 survey of AUB students at a time when he was on trial for bombing a church. However, Ja'ja', convicted and already sentenced for life, was barely mentioned in the 1996 survey of LU students. In both instances, the media played a key role.

In 1993, Hariri was a newcomer to the premiership and a lot of hope was pinned on his perceived ability to create a drastic economic and political transformation. His projected image then was that of a savior capable of miraculously transiting Lebanon from a state of chaos, destruction, and misery to stable peace, busting construction, and sustained prosperity. The media portrayed Hariri as a man who could obliterate the profound anguish of demoralization and despair the Lebanese had developed, and they created an air of genuine hope and ever-lasting bliss. In sharp contrast, the image of Ja'ja' was that of a terrorist, political assassin, and mass murderer of church attendants.

By the same token, the media, in 1993, painted Aoun's character as a dissenting insurgent who would spare no human lives to destabilize the country. He was labeled a "small general" charged with keeping millions of dollars of public donations to himself while claiming to be honest and decent. Such alleged negative attributes must have won him the hatred of many students, particularly Muslims, who had also tasted the bitter flavor of his mortar shells in 1989 when he traded heavy artillery fire with the Syrian army. Despite his negative image in the media, Aoun has other personal and political qualities that have won him the love of many Christians, as elaborated later in the chapter.

Religious sect is probably the most important acquired affiliation that determines one's choice of liked or hated leaders. Survey findings show a strong trend among students to select their most preferred leaders from their own religion or sect, and their most disliked leaders from other sects.[12] To some extent, the Orthodox parliamentarian Najah Wakim is an exception to the rule in being the second most popular leader among Christians in general and among Shiite Muslims as well.

At LU, the most liked leaders for the majority of Christians, Druze, and over 40% of Sunni and Shiite students were from their own sect or religion (table 7.2). Yet, a significant percentage of Sunnis and Shiites selected leaders from other sects, or named historical figures like Gamal Abdel-Nasser. Of the selected leaders, Aoun was most popular among Christians, particularly Maronites (34% of Maronites named him). It is also likely that Aoun is relatively popular among other segments of the Christian population, particularly Maronites.

The continuous relative popularity of Aoun among Christians can be attributed to several factors:

- Many Christians believe that the Syrians were behind their "defeat" in the civil war and their current subdued and depressed state (*ihbat*). Aoun was the only Maronite leader that resisted any Syrian role in Lebanon and maintained an uncompromising stand toward them even after being forced into exile. His military confrontation with the Syrian army in 1989 won him the admiration of Christians despite his military and political blunders that inflicted heavy destruction in their residential areas and eventually resulted in his defeat and exile.

- Many Maronites, perhaps most, are still unable to comprehend the fact that their dominance of Lebanon has irrevocably ended, regardless of the Syrian presence. Their demographic, political, and economic weights have all receded.[13] The only way they can regain the dominance they once enjoyed in pre-war Lebanon is through an armed revolt that would establish a totalitarian, terrorist regime that suffocates the majority of its citizens. Such a regime does not bode well for the democracy-loving Lebanese, let alone its slim chances of long life. On the other hand, the substantial share allocated to Maronites in the Taif document is quite larger than what their demographic and economic weights justify.[14] Some Maronite politicians, such as Hrawi and the Minister of Foreign Affairs, Faris Bouez, seemingly cognizant of these demographic and economic facts, have thrown their full support behind the Taif accord.

- Almost all the Christian opposition politicians who lost their influence or positions in the political system rally around Aoun in order to strengthen their positions in negotiating a return to political life. With those interests in mind, they use all kinds of maneuvers and misinformation to incite Christians against the regime.

- Young students tend to favor aggressive, outspoken, extremist leaders more than the moderate and timid. Aoun's character somewhat fits these sought-after attributes.

Hariri was most liked by the Sunni students (32% named him). Not only is Hariri relatively popular among Sunni students, but also among his Sunni constituency in Beirut, as evidenced in the 1996 parliamentary elections. In Chapter 4 elaborates on his present status as the most influential and popular leader among Sunnis. The Druze students chose Minister Walid Junblat as their most favored leader (23% named him). There is no doubt that Junblat remains much more

Table 7.2: Most Liked Leader by Student's Sect, LU 1996

CATEGORY OF LEADER	STUDENT'S RELIGIOUS SECT (%)					
	Maronite	Catholic	Orthodox	Sunni	Shiite	Druze
Same Sect	9	2	18	41	43	58
Different Sect, Same Religion	16	79	68	4	10	7
Different Religion	7	9	5	18	20	16
Regional Leader	0	2	2	4	8	0
International Leader	4	0	2	5	2	3
Other: Historical, Nonpolitical	1	4	0	20	14	16
None	3	4	5	4	3	0
Total	**100**	**100**	**100**	**100**	**100**	**100**
No. of students	**226**	**57**	**60**	**114**	**239**	**62**

influential among the Druze than his rival, Arslan. Hizbullah leaders were most liked by the Shiites (25% named one of them), a sign of their impressive power base among students and other Shiites as well.

As previously stated, the majority of students did not express hatred or dislike for any particular political leader. Yet, most disliked among LU students of all sects but Sunnis was Hariri (table 7.3). The percentage of students who disliked him ranged from a high value of 43% among Catholics and 37% among the Shiites to fewer than 10% among Sunnis. The attitudes of students are likely to reflect general attitudes of their religious communities towards Hariri. The overwhelming majority of Sunnis either support him or refrain from attacking him, while significant proportions of the other religious communities dislike him along with other members of his cabinet, notably, Murr. One can explain the resentment of non-Sunni students toward Hariri in terms of:

- His domineering character and prominent role in the regime as a Sunni. He has often overshadowed the heads of the other sects. The Maronites and the Catholics yearn for the old days when their co-religionist leaders played an overbearing role in the Lebanese polity. The Shiites abhor the rise of a powerful Sunni prime minister since he might prevent them from expanding their share of political power, or even act to curtail it. In the postwar polity, all Muslim sects combined are eligible to half the parliamentary seats and half the top administrative positions. Within the Muslim quota, Shiites, Sunnis, and Druze have to agree on their respective shares, which results in continuous disputes among them. Competition is particularly fierce between Sunni and Shiite leaders over certain coveted positions because they feel that their enhanced power in postwar Lebanon must be maintained and expanded if and when possible.

- His drive toward strengthening the central government which the Lebanese have traditionally distrusted. The army and the security forces are now capable of enforcing law and order after 16 years of chaos. Under Hariri, the cabinet has introduced many new laws and regulations making the lives of people more complicated than before and has levied new taxes on all sorts of commodities and services. Higher indirect taxes have won Hariri the anger and resentment of most lower and middle-class people. Strict security measures and alleged coercion during the 1996 parliamentary elections have made the Minister of Interior the second most disliked person by LU students from all sects.

- The economic problems that many people continue to face despite the end of civil strife. Dissipated is the once-held illusion that Hariri's economic policy would drastically improve the lives of the poor and the middle classes. Under his rampant capitalism, the poor are getting poorer and the rich richer. By constantly exposing this problem to the public, the opposition deputy Najah Wakim succeeded in gaining the sympathy and support of a large segment of the Lebanese, including Muslims and students.

Table 7.3: Most Disliked Leader by Student's Sect, LU 1996

CATEGORY OF LEADER	STUDENT'S RELIGIOUS SECT (%)					
	Maronite	Catholic	Orthodox	Sunni	Shiite	Druze
Same Sect	20	0	12	10	6	2
Different Sect, Same Religion	22	34	23	18	41	25
Different Religion	40	52	45	34	27	43
Regional Leader	7	8	5	29	17	20
International Leader	1	0	3	1	4	4
Other: Historical, Nonpolitical	0	0	0	0	0	0
None	4	0	5	2	2	2
All Politicians	7	6	7	6	3	4
Total	**100**	**100**	**100**	**100**	**100**	**100**
No. of students	**95**	**49**	**113**	**258**	**146**	**63**

At AUB in 1993, as in LU in 1996, the same names of liked leaders featured in the students' responses, yet with lower percentages of supporters. Aoun was named most liked by 28% of Maronite students and Hariri by 20% of Sunni students. Unlike LU students, most AUB students did not name leaders from their sect or religion. The answers were spread out over the categories "same sect," "different sect, same religion," "different religion," and "historical or nonpolitical figures" (tables 7.4 and 7.5). A large proportion of students from each of the sects looked up to a historical or nonpolitical famous character, a finding that was explained earlier in the chapter.

Table 7.4: Most Liked Leader by Student's Sect, AUB 1993

CATEGORY OF LEADER	STUDENT'S RELIGIOUS SECT (%)					
	Maronite	Catholic	Orthodox	Sunni	Shiite	Druze
Same Sect	42	2	0	33	28	25
Different Sect, Same Religion	3	37	44	1	12	15
Different Religion	5	4	4	5	7	14
Regional Leader	2	2	4	15	17	9
International Leader	13	14	18	7	8	11
Other: Historical, Nonpolitical	29	35	27	35	23	18
None	6	6	3	5	5	8
Total	**100**	**100**	**100**	**100**	**100**	**100**
No. of Students	**96**	**49**	**113**	**265**	**145**	**63**

It is worth noting that in both surveys (1993 and 1996), and also in the 1997 survey by al-Amin and Faour, none of the Lebanese politicians reached the status of a national leader since none garnered the support of a majority of Lebanese students. Also, none of the non-Lebanese politicians were selected as the most liked leader by a majority of students. In other words, students identified neither with any local politician, nor with any of the world's politicians. By contrast, in the pre-war period, Hanf found a different group of preferred local leaders, one of whom was favored by a large proportion of students. Former deputy, Raymond Eddeh, was most preferred by students (45% of LU students and 37% of AUB students) followed by Camille Chamoun and then Kamal Junblat.[15] Among the international leaders, the late President De

Table 7.5: Most Disliked Leader Student's Sect, AUB 1993

CATEGORY OF LEADER	STUDENT'S RELIGIOUS SECT (%)					
	Maronite	Catholic	Orthodox	Sunni	Shiite	Druze
Same Sect	46	0	0	3	7	2
Different Sect, Same Religion	1	40	34	25	3	11
Different Religion	12	6	8	9	37	43
Regional Leader	10	18	20	27	25	8
International Leader	16	18	22	20	14	18
Other: Historical, Nonpolitical	4	10	11	8	8	10
None	10	2	5	5	3	8
All Politicians	2	6	0	3	3	0
Total	100	100	100	100	100	100
No. of Students	95	49	113	258	146	63

Gaulle of France was most favored by both LU and AUB students (27% and 24%, respectively), followed by the Chinese revolutionary Mao Tseh Tung and the Egyptian pan-Arab leader Gamal Abdel Nasser. In other words, comparing the pre-war with the postwar periods, one can infer that a lot more students at that time had political role models.

The absence of role models in Lebanese politics reflects the students' mistrust of local politicians, persistence of sectarian politics, and diffusion of political leadership. With the exception of Najah Wakim, the relatively popular politicians (Aoun, Hariri, Junblat, and Nasrallah/Fadlallah) are popular only within their sect. Moreover, almost all sectarian leaderships are more divided now than ever before. Neither

Aoun among the Maronites, nor Hariri among the Sunnis, nor Junblat among the Druze received a majority vote from students. Results of the 1996 parliamentary elections point to the same conclusion. For each religious community, one finds at least two leaders, none of whom has a dominant appeal to his constituency. Either may assume more power than the other at any given time depending on a variety of internal and external factors.

Defects in the Polity

College students of Lebanon are cognizant of systemic defects in their nation's political system. A large segment, ranging from half the students at AUB in 1993 to the large majority of LU students in 1996, were generally dissatisfied with the nature of the postwar polity and the performance of its functionaries. In 1993, a quarter of AUB students wished to see Lebanon a "democratic, secular state," 17% wanted to see sectarianism abolished from politics, and 10% called for more radical change.[16] In 1996, the overwhelming majority of LU students (82%) wished to have a better political system, half of whom specified freedom of opinion and expression, and equality of opportunity as desired features.

Desire for radical action among AUB students is only significantly related to political orientation. While 20% of the Islamists adopted radical change in the political system, only 10% of the Lebanese nationalists and 7% of the Arab nationalists wanted that sort of change. Put differently, most alienated from the political system in Lebanon are the Islamists.

Corruption was reported as a major reason for LU students' discontent with the government. Most (88%) felt insecure about their future in Lebanon for what they perceived as corruption of public officers who favor their private interests over those of the public (50%).[17] "Fiefdom" (*mazra'a*) is the pejorative term that is frequently invoked to describe the prevalence of corruption, patronage, and nepotism in the state. Many students published their written assessment of the Lebanese political system in the widely circulated weekly publication *Nahar Ashabab*. Using an indirect style of description, a student wrote the following about the Lebanese state entitled, *"Mazra'a"*:

> A prosperous state, bountiful and wealthy...Its most common 'produce'
> are sectarianism, bribery, corruption, and treachery. Its economy is

based on renewable natural resources such as growing of hashish and opium (whose production is gradually in decline).[18]

The most important reason for LU students' discontent with the government is what they viewed as bad economic conditions in Lebanon and bleak employment prospects.   Many expressed their dismay at the regime's disregard for the needs and opinions of the youth.   In the words of one student:

> How long should we wait?
> Isn't it dangerous to think that we have no future here in our homeland? They [alluding to rulers] call upon the emigrants to return home. Why? Nothing is guaranteed. And if we have missed the train of stability and decent living, what awaits our little children? What have we prepared for them but an 'archive' full of ruins and remains? Don't they deserve better than being treated like computers that are programmed to suit our obsolete vision?[19]

Nevertheless, LU students valued the government's priority goal of establishing law and order in the country. When asked to name three major obligations the government has towards its citizens, the most important obligation named was security (51%), followed by protecting freedom of opinion and expression (39%).

The single most important factor that influences students' approval or disapproval of government policy is religious sect. In 1994, AUB students were asked to assess the performance of the Hariri government on a five-point scale from excellent to very bad. A minority gave the government a bad or very bad mark (16%), but there was substantial variation by sect. Maronite students, whose community has repeatedly expressed its dissatisfaction with the post Taif regime, were most critical of the government; close to one third gave it a "bad" or "very bad" score on performance. By contrast, only 6% of the Sunnis and 13% of the Druze shared their evaluation.[20]

At LU in 1996, as in AUB in 1994, there were differences between Maronite and Sunni students regarding their disposition toward Hariri's cabinet. The new element in the LU findings is that the majority of students expressed negative attitudes toward the Hariri government regardless of sect. The proportion of students who felt insecure about their future in Lebanon because of the poor government performance ranged from a large 71% among the Sunnis to above 90% among the other sects, at times reaching 97%. More importantly, the students

Table 7.6: Political Ideological Orientation of Students by University and Year

STUDENT'S IDEOLOGY	1970* (%) AUB	LU	1993 (%)
Lebanese Nationalism	25	26	68
Syrian Nationalism	5	9	3
Arab Nationalism	33	40	16
Internationalism (1970)/ Islamism (1993)	23	17	8
Total %	**100**	**100**	**100**

*Source: Barakat, 1977, Appendix, p. 208. Note that all LU students were Lebanese while 52% of AUB students were Lebanese and 48% other Arabs.

expressed their willingness to act in order to remedy the situation. Close to 90% of the Maronite students versus 79% of the Sunnis accepted to do something to change the status quo. However, the students had no clear, explicit plans for change and did not ponder or pledge to take any specific steps to that effect.

Political Orientation

In 1993, the majority of Lebanese students at AUB considered themselves to be Lebanese nationalists irrespective of their gender, religion, academic major, or social class. In 1970, Barakat found LU students divided among three political orientations: Lebanese nationalism, Arab nationalism, and internationalism—i.e, socialism and communism (table 7.6). In 1970, Arab nationalism had a lot more adherents among Muslims, particularly Sunnis, than among Christians, a finding that still holds today as well (figure 7.1). Historically, Muslims, particularly Sunnis, identified with the Arab nation and Arab causes more than the other religious groups. This ideological gap between Muslims and Christians has not vanished after the end of the civil war, but it has narrowed down considerably.

Lebanese nationalism attracted more males than females (figure 7.2), perhaps because girls tend to comply with the prevalent values and

Figure 7.1: Political Orientations of AUB Students by Religious Sect

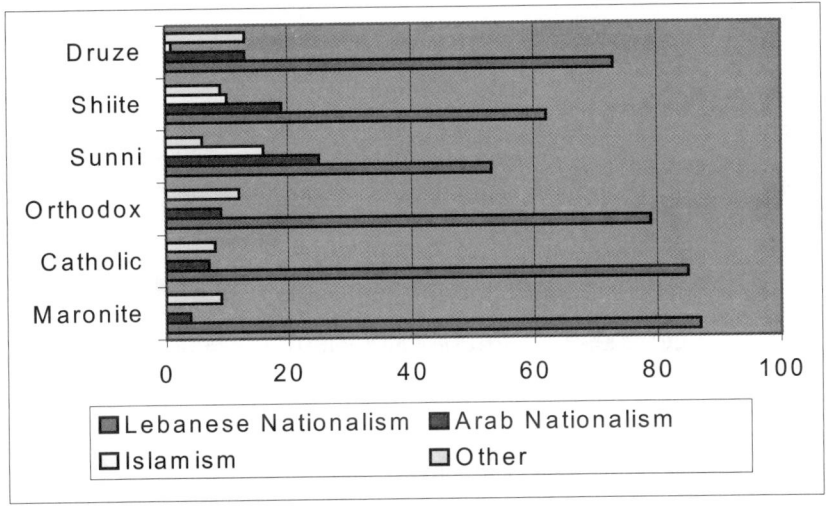

Figure 7.2: Political Orientations of AUB Students by Gender

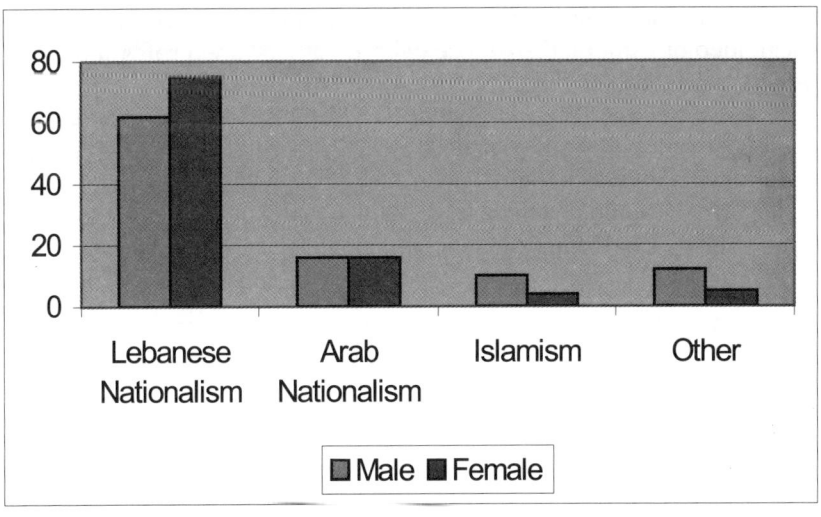

Figure 7.3: Political Orientations of AUB Students by Social Class

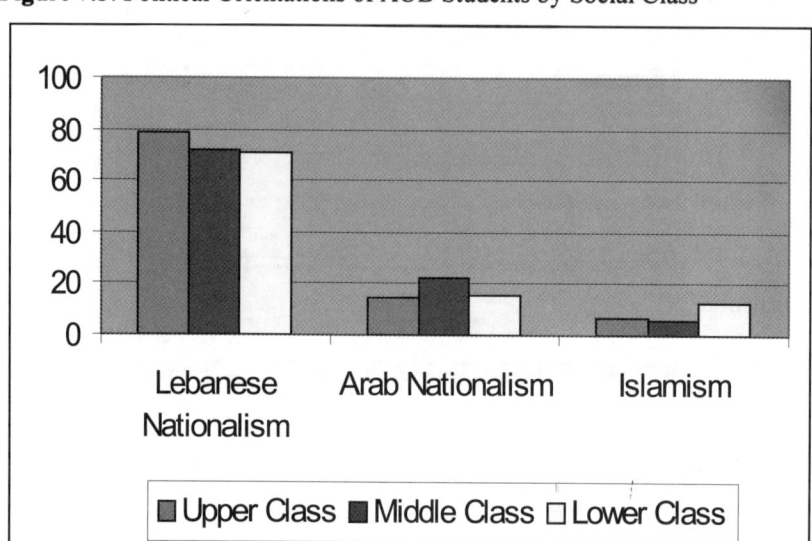

norms of the dominant political ideology.[21]   Support for Lebanese nationalism also varied with social class.   Students whose fathers are business owners and managers tended to adopt Lebanese nationalism as a political ideology more than those whose fathers are professionals or employees and workers (figure 7.3).   Apparently, the economic interests of Lebanese business entrepreneurs calls for the adherence to territorial nationalism, while the professionals' economic survival and prosperity calls for more openness to the Arab world and regional integration.

One can infer a similar change among LU students on the basis of their selection of the most liked political leader.   The majority selected local politicians who espouse Lebanese nationalism.   On the other hand, Islamism attracted students from lower and lower-middle class backgrounds—children of workers and employees—more than from the higher classes (Figure 7.3).

This shift in ideological orientation is a reflection of a more general trend in Lebanon and other Arab countries.   Since the Camp David Accords were signed in 1978, Arab nationalism/pan-Arabism has been experiencing a steady decline.   Its demise allowed territorial nationalism, or *qutriyya* (such as Lebanese, Egyptian, or Palestinian nationalism), and Islamism to sweep across the Arab world.   Territorial nationalism was openly endorsed by most Arab states and implicitly adopted by all, while Islamism became the ideology of popular dissent among the alienated and the repressed.[22]

The dominance of Lebanese nationalism as a political ideology among students is a testimony to the wide acceptance of the Taif accord's clause on national identity (see Chapter 4).   If students—the more liberal and radical elements of the Lebanese—have come to identify themselves with Lebanese nationalism, then it is more likely that the Lebanese layman today clings to that identity too.

Sectarianism

To gauge the strength of their confessional loyalties, AUB students were asked a series of questions in 1993.   The questions dealt with issues such as students' choices concerning friends, mates, residential neighborhood, and attitudes toward other sects.   The findings showed that a majority (62%) expressed strong attachment to their religious sect, and preferred to get married to someone from their sect— 66% (table 7.7).   The closest friend of most students belonged to their religion.   For the majority of Muslim students (half the Shiites and 60% of the Sunnis), their best friends belonged to their religious sect (table 7.8).

As for inter-sectarian relations, contrary to Khashan's findings,[23] most AUB students did not show hostile attitudes toward other sects, did not support their sects unconditionally, and favored the institution of civil marriage in the country.   On the issue of civil marriage, there is a Muslim-Christian difference that surfaced in the students' answers.   Least supportive of it were the Sunnis (48% approved its institution) followed by the Shiites (57%).   Most supportive were the Druze (78%).   This variation is caused by the degree of religiosity of students.[24]   Believers in God who were regular observers of religious rituals tended to disapprove of civil marriage (67%), while believers who do not practice religious rites favored it (75%).   Most enthusiastic about civil marriage were the non-believers or atheists (98%).

The negative attitude of religious students toward the institution of civil marriage can be explained in terms of their doctrinal beliefs.

Table 7.7: Percentage of AUB Students who Agree with Each of the Following Statements on Confessional Ties*

QUESTION	% AGREE OR % YES
I believe that my sect can serve Lebanon better than any other sect	33
My sect is superior to all other sects	23
I am strongly attached to my sect	62
One should live among people of his sect	18
Do you prefer to live in a neighborhood where most residents belong to your religious sect?	19
Do you usually buy goods from shops that are owned by people belonging to your sect?	2
If your sect gets in conflict with members of another sect, would you support your sect without question or reservation?	22
Lebanon should become a secular state (i.e., religious affiliation should not affect appointments in public positions)	82
Do you prefer to get married to a person who belongs to your religious sect?	66
Civil marriage should be instituted in Lebanon	59

*Number of students is 793.

Religious denominations tend to encourage their followers to associate with and marry members of their own denomination. The objective is to integrate their religious community and tighten up its internal cohesiveness, while inter-faith marriages tend to dilute the bond between believers of the same sect. Although the institution of civil marriage would not stop the current practice of conducting marriage ceremonies by the clergy, it would certainly remove a legal and practical barrier for

Table 7.8: Religious Sect of Closest Friend by Student's Sect, AUB 1993

SECT OF CLOSEST FRIEND	STUDENT'S RELIGIOUS SECT (%)					
	Maronite	Catholic	Orthodox	Sunni	Shiite	Druze
Same Sect	46	22	35	60	49	38
Same Religion, Different Sect	27	55	33	24	33	42
Different Religion	27	23	32	16	18	20
Total	100	100	100	100	100	100
No. of students	99	49	116	269	145	64

those desiring to have civil marriage.

A statistical analysis was employed to test the relationship between religiosity and approval of civil marriage while controlling for the effect of religious sect. Within each sect, approval of civil marriage was inversely related to religiosity. The more religious a student was, regardless of his/her sect, the less supportive of civil marriage he/she would be (table 7.9). This association was most significant among the Sunnis and the Shiites (level of statistical significance = 0.001). Moreover, both gender and political ideology had no bearing on the relationship between religiosity and attitude toward civil marriage. A multivariate, logistic regression analysis was employed to test the additive effects of gender, sect, political orientation, and religiosity on whether or not civil marriage was approved. The result showed that the effect of religiosity on the attitude toward civil marriage is significant, net of the effects of all the other independent variables combined (table A). Indeed, religiosity is the only predictor that retains significance when all the other variables are included in the regression equation.

The students' views of "confessional bureaucracy" were explicitly negative. The overwhelming majority (82%) supported an end to the practice of sectarian allocation of public positions (table 7.7). The only significant correlate of this variable was religiosity: the less religious, the more supportive of ending sectarianism. While 72% of the

Table 7.9: Percentage of AUB Students who Approve of Civil Marriage by Religiosity and Sect, 1993

RELIGIOUS SECT	RELIGIOSITY			Level of Sig.
	Regular Observer of Rites	Occasional Observer of Rites	Believer, Non-Observer of Rites	
Maronite	40 (35)	57 (28)	75 (28)	.05
Catholic	36 (14)	57 (14)	82 (17)	.05
Orthodox	48 (23)	68 (25)	82 (49)	.05
Sunni	29 (109)	46 (69)	66 (74)	.001
Shiite	29 (52)	52 (23)	73 (60)	.001
Druze	–	–	76 (50)	Not applicable

– less than 5 cases.
() numbers between parentheses refer to the number of cases.

Note: Nonbelievers were excluded because their few numbers create unstable values of chi-square. However, the percentages of supporters of civil marriage among nonbelievers within each sect, where their numbers are large enough to warrant computing a percentage, are the highest.

regular observers of rites endorsed the abolition of confessionalism in government, the corresponding percentage among nonbelievers was 92%.

In response to the question: "Do you prefer to live in a neighborhood where most residents belong to your religious sect," the overwhelming majority of AUB students (81%) said no (table 7.7). This proclivity for religious desegregation is in line with the observed decline in geographic segregation of religious communities since 1990. Many people who fled religiously-mixed neighborhoods during the war have returned to their original domiciles, and many newly weds are taking up residence in suburbs that are inhabited by people from other sects. In comparison with pre-war Lebanon, most communities still exhibit religious homogeneity and usually sectarian homogeneity as well.

To examine the correlates of sectarianism, a summary measure, or index of sectarianism, was constructed. The index consisted of eight items from table 7.7 and an additional ninth item.[25] It ranged from 0 as the lowest value to 8 as the highest. The average value of the index was 2.5, which is a relatively low value indicating a low level of sectarianism among AUB students. The median was 2.0 out of 8.0, which means that half the students had scores below 2 and half above 2, another indication of limited sectarianism. The percentage of students scoring 0 was a substantial 19% indicating no sectarian feelings and ties.

Confessional ties were significantly associated with a number of socioeconomic and political factors, notably, religiosity, sect, social class, and political ideology. As for religiosity, it varied positively with confessional ties. The more religious a person was, the more attached to his/her religious community he/she became (table 7.10). It is expected that people who are tightly knit to their religious community through rituals would develop intense sectarian feelings and loyalty. One important contributing factor to these intense feelings is that each religious doctrine in Lebanon emphasizes its distinctiveness from the other doctrines even when they belong to the same religion. Therefore, a rise in the prevalence of religiosity in a community implies higher intensity of sectarian feelings and loyalties at the expense of national allegiance.

Religion is reported to have played an important or very important role in the lives of the majority of college students in 1996. Although important to both, more LU than AUB students had strong positive feelings about religion (table 7.11). This difference may be attributed to LU students' lower and lower-middle class background and their rural origins; lower classes and rural people tend to exhibit higher levels of religiosity than their upper class and urban counterparts. Also, more women than men viewed religion to be important to them (table 7.11). The largest proportion of students who regarded religion as important or very important in their lives was among LU females (86%),

Table 7.10: Mean of Sectarianism by Political Ideology and Religiosity
AUB, 1993

			N	**Mean**
Variable	**Ideology**	1 Lebanese Nationalism	510	2.50
		2 Arab Nationalism	122	2.05
		3 Syrian Nationalism	20	0.55
		4 Islamism	57	4.68
	Religiosity	1 Believer & Regularly Practices	228	3.59
		2 Believer & Occasionally Practices	158	2.62
		3 Believer & Does Not Practice	271	1.92
		4 Non Believer	52	0.96
	War Experience*	1 None	207	2.78
		2 Low Level of Suffering	327	2.57
		3 High Level of Suffering	242	2.15

Grand Mean=2.56

---

*This index is composed of the summation of scores on the following three questions:
1. Were you ever displaced because of the war for more than 6 consecutive months? Yes=1, No=0
2. Were you injured/kidnapped during the war? Yes=1, No=0
3. Was any family member or friend injured/kidnapped during the war? Yes=1, No=0.

Thus, the index ranges from 0 to 3: "0" refers to the absence of negative experience due to war, "1" to a low level of suffering, and the combined categories "2" and "3" to a high level of suffering. The categories "2" and "3" were combined because of a negligible variation in sectarianism between the two.

while the lowest proportion was among AUB males with 55% (table 7.11).

Gender differences in religiosity has been documented in several other studies.[26] Women are more religious than men because religiosity is associated with pro-social attitudes that are more prevalent among women.[27] Every major religion preaches compassion and helpfulness, qualities that more women possess than do men. Women have consistently been found to be more caring, empathic, helping, and compassionate than are men.[28] Women tend to show positive social behavior, like promoting group solidarity, while men tend to show negative social behavior, like competitiveness, disagreement, and aggression.[29]

At LU, the prevalence of religiosity has risen dramatically since 1971 (table 7.12). Between 1971 and 1996, the percentage of students stating that religion has a strong influence on their lives more than doubled, reaching 53% of total students. Among AUB students, the corresponding percentage was 23%. Despite the absence of baseline data from the pre-war era, it can be argued, based on the survey data of this study, that the degree of religiosity among AUB students has been on the decline since the end of the war. In 1996, the percentage of students who were regular observers of religious rites was 18%, down from 31% in 1993. Thus, in comparison to pre-war Lebanon, the postwar results imply an increase in the degree of sectarianism among LU students and a decrease among AUB students.

The divergent temporal trend in sectarianism between AUB and LU may be attributed to a host of factors that characterize their different "habituses." One such factor is the nature of the university's physical setting. AUB has one campus while LU has multiple campuses, each housing students from the same religion, and in some cases the same sect, leading to their isolation from other sects. This isolation is likely to nurture parochial feelings and loyalties and adverse attitudes toward those religious groups with which students do not interact. The lack of continuous social interaction breeds misinformation, reinforces misconception, and fosters rigid positions. Such a situation hampers efforts at resolving current or future disputes between social communities. In the theory and practice of conflict resolution, parties in dispute are always encouraged to get to the negotiation table and stay in contact with each other even if a war is raging between them.

Table 7.11: Religiosity of Lebanese Students by University and Sex, 1996

Importance of Religion in Student's Life	AUB (%)		LU (%)	
	Male	Female	Male	Female
Not Important	22	13	7	3
Neutral	23	24	14	11
Important or Very Important	55	63	79	86
No. of students	299	340	385	611
X^2	8.8		10.1	
Df	2		2	
Prob. Value	.012		<.01	

Table 7.12: Religiosity of Lebanese Students by University and Year

Influence of Religious Faith in One's Life	LU (%)		AUB (%)
	1971*	1996	1996
Little Influence/Not Important & Neutral	33	17	41
Some Influence/Important	36	30	36
High Influence/Very Important	23	53	23
Number of Students	219	1029	641

*Source: Barakat, 1977, Appendix, pp. 206-207

The nature of academic relations between students and faculty is another contributing factor to the trends in sectarianism at AUB and LU. At AUB, faculty members keep regular office hours and are in constant interaction with their students, who are also encouraged to think critically and voice their opinions openly even when in disagreement with the instructor's views. At LU, the faculty members rarely keep office hours, if at all, and most only show up on campus to lecture. Usually, established older professors have other jobs to attend to. The instructor's only duty, in practice, is to deliver lectures to a large audience with limited interaction and feedback from the students. Students are socialized to digest what is dictated to them without much critical evaluation. The obvious consequence is rigid thinking and limited exposure to new ideas, a recipe for parochialism and intense sectarian feelings.

A third factor that explains the different trends in sectarianism between AUB and LU is the rural origin of most LU students, who also have lower class backgrounds, while AUB students are mostly urban with middle and upper class backgrounds. Furthermore, a significant proportion of the Lebanese students at AUB have completed their high school education abroad, mainly in American and British schools where Western values prevail. In a rural setting, primordial ties such as sectarianism flourish. When rural students enroll in a university, their values and loyalties also relocate to the college campus.

The last factor that influences sectarianism relates to administrative and financial aspects. LU is a public university under the control of the government. The dependence of LU on the Lebanese political system renders it vulnerable to sectarian politics and to the whims of ministers and members of the ruling troika. This is manifested in a variety of practices, notably, nepotism, meddling of sectarian politics in university affairs, and limited accountability of administrators. In such a setting, rather than dislodge primordial loyalties, education at LU is more likely to reinforce them. By contrast, AUB is a private, nonprofit institution that is independent of any government or organization. A president and a host of administrators, who are accountable to an independent board of trustees, manage AUB. Members of this board have a diversity of social, educational, and national backgrounds.

In addition to varying by university, sectarianism also varies with father's occupation. The data reveal that least sectarian were the children of professionals and most sectarian were the children of business owners and managers. However, father's occupation, or social class, explained only 1% of the variation in sectarianism, which makes it a negligible predictor of sectarianism.

The extent of suffering due to acts of war is also related to the intensity of sectarianism. Students who suffered displacement from their homes for an extended period (6 months or more in this survey) might have developed antagonistic feelings towards the other religious groups if these groups were perceived as their source of displacement. Those who were injured during the fighting, kidnapped, or witnessed the injury or kidnapping of a family member or friend, are also likely to develop negative attitudes toward other sects. An index that measures the students' experience with such atrocities of war was constructed, then its relationship with sectarianism tested. The data show that as the extent of suffering increased, students became less sectarian. The statistical association is significant at the 0.05 level, but like father's occupation, it explains fewer than 2% of the total variations in sectarianism.

Political ideology, which includes Lebanese nationalism, Arab nationalism, Syrian nationalism, and Islamism, had a considerable bearing on confessional feelings and ties. These ties were most tight among Islamists and most loose among believers in Syrian nationalism (table 7.10). Not surprisingly, political Islam heightens one's feelings of belonging to one religious community that stands out in stark contrast to all other communities. *Dar al-Islam,* to Islamists, is the bode of believers that is totally different from societies that are not ruled according to the Islamic law *shari'a.* Such societies are considered similar to the *Jahiliyya* or pre-Islamic society that Islam managed to change.

Unlike the Islamist ideology, Syrian nationalism calls for the integration of different religious communities in a unified, secular state namely that of Greater Syria. Hence, it is *ipso facto* not hospitable to sectarianism, which explains why students with pan-Syrian orientation scored very low on sectarianism. The ideology of Syrian nationalism is strictly and explicitly secular. As for pan-Arab students who endorsed Arab unity under one state, they differed appreciably from pan-Syrian students though they had the second lowest score on sectarianism (table 7.10). This result is understandable in view of the different strands of Arab nationalism; many Arab nationalists are secular while others are not. For example, religious Muslims who subscribe to pan-Arabism see no point in the secularization of an Arab state since most of its population would be Muslims of the same denomination. Lebanese nationalists, on the other hand, had a "middle of the road" score on sectarianism because this group is more heterogeneous than the pan-Arab group. The non-secular elements within the ranks of Lebanese nationalists include fundamentalist Christians and many fundamentalist Muslims.

When examined jointly in a statistical analysis, both religiosity and political ideology determined the level of sectarianism among AUB students. Religiosity, however, is more important; it, alone, explains 18% of the total variation in sectarianism, while the two factors combined explain 24% (table A11).[30]

Inter-Sectarian Relations

The data permit an evaluation of the degree of social distance among the various sects. Respondents were requested to identify the sect that was closest to their own and the one that was most distant. The end product of this exercise is a political map of coalitions among religious sects (tables 7.13; A12; A13). Closest to Maronites were Catholics, and the Shiites were most distant. The Shiites were also most distant from the two other Christian sects, Catholics and Orthodox. Catholics were closest to both Maronites and Orthodox, while the Orthodox were closest only to the Catholics. Besides feeling most distant from the Shiites, the Orthodox also felt distant from the Druze.

Among Muslims, Sunnis and Shiites were perceived to be closest to each other, and most distant from the Maronites followed by the Druze. An interesting finding is that the Druze felt isolated from all other sects: the highest percentage of Druze students stated: "No sect is closest." This reveals a profound sense of distrust by the Druze in other religious groups as a result of their recurrent conflicts with the Maronites and occasional conflicts with the Sunnis and Shiites. Most distant from the Druze were the Maronites, which is an expected finding in view of the bitter, bloody, historical experience between the Druze and the Maronites in Mount Lebanon.

In light of the above, one can state that close, friendly relations exist among sects of the same religion and unfriendly, distrustful relations among sects of different religions. The only exception to this generalization on inter-sectarian relations is the Druze, who are neither Christians, nor full-fledged Muslims, for much of their religion's rituals and beliefs are secretive. Notwithstanding, distance between pairs of sects of the same religion, such as Shiites and Druze or Orthodox and

Table 7.13: Percentage of Parents Upset with AUB Students Over Staying Out Late by Religion, 1994

	Maronite	Catholic	Orthodox	Sunni	Shiite	Druze
Maronite		C1		D1	D1	D1
Catholic	C1		C1			
Orthodox		C1				
Sunni						
Shiite	D1	D1	D1		C1	C2
Druze			D2	D2	D2	
None is Close						C1

Table 7.14: Students' Opinions Regarding Naturalization of the Palestinians by Relgious Sect, AUB 1993

	Maronite	Orthodox	Other Christian	Sunni	Shiite	Druze	Total
% Oppose	72	62	69	59	75	55	64
Number of Students	98	118	68	227	150	67	778

Maronites, are not insignificant, yet not as wide as between sects of different religions. To be sure, social distance is neither solely, nor mainly, a function of similarity in religious beliefs. Rather, it is rooted in the history of inter-sectarian relations that are shaped by economic and political interests.

Naturalization of Palestinians

The Palestinian presence in Lebanon used to be a divisive, explosive issue in domestic politics. Every time it was brought up for discussion, emotions flared up between Muslims and Christians. Since the end of civil strife, Muslim politicians have adopted a new position regarding this issue, which brought them closer to the pre-war Maronite position.

The data show that the majority of AUB students in 1993 (64%) opposed naturalization of resident Palestinians, a proposal that was in circulation at the wake of the civil war. As expected, the attitudes of these students varied with sect. Most sympathetic were the Druze, followed by the Sunnis (table 7.14). The affinity between the Palestinians and the Druze goes back to the civil war days when both were bound together in a military and political alliance under the leadership of both Yasser Arafat and the late Kamal Junblat. Junblat was the uncontested head of the Lebanese "nationalist and progressive" parties and forces, while Arafat had both military and financial power. The Palestinian guerrillas proved faithful allies to the Druze during their battles with the Maronite Lebanese Forces in 1983.

The sympathy of a large segment of the Sunnis for the Palestinians emanates from at least two principal reasons. First, most of the Palestinians are Sunnis and both communities have supported each other since the arrival of the first wave of Palestinian refugees in 1948. Second, for many Sunnis, loyalty to pan-Arab orientation demands the support of Arab causes. Besides Arab unity, the Palestinian cause has loomed large on the agenda of pan-Arab politics since the establishment of Israel in 1948.

Vehement opposition to Palestinian naturalization came from both Maronites and Shiites since both are afraid that the addition of some 300,000 Sunnis would tip the sectarian balance in favor of Sunnis for many years down the line. Many students openly expressed that concern, while others mentioned the likelihood of losing jobs to cheaper

Palestinian labor. Others believed that such a step would weaken the Palestinian resolve to return to their occupied homeland. These attitudes mirror a general negative feeling toward Palestinians among influential politicians, which also coincides with the government's position. In 1995, when Minister Walid Junblat suggested to the government to provide decent housing for the refugees, all hell broke loose because of its political implications. In response, he had to abandon the whole idea.

Summary

Most AUB and LU students had no role models among the local politicians. The majority of LU students were dissatisfied with the political system and the performance of the government and felt insecure about their future in Lebanon. At AUB, a majority of students expressed strong feelings toward their religious sect but did not report hostile attitudes toward other sects or said they would support their sects unconditionally.

In their assessment of inter-sectarian relations, AUB students believed that sects that belong to the same religion had close relations with one another, whereas sects that belong to different religions had distant relations from one another. As to their attitude toward the naturalization of the Palestinians, most AUB students opposed it, particularly the Maronites and Shiites.

CHAPTER 8

CHANGING NORMS: IMPLICATIONS AND SUGGESTIONS

> The time of national awakening in Lebanon's
> history shall be when we abolish sectarianism.
>
> Riad Solh[1]

This book has examined the prevalence of a host of social norms and values among college students in Lebanon. At the individual level, students scored high on the value of individualism and low on the value of authoritarianism. The levels of both values compare favorably with Western societies. Although no comparable pre-war data are available, it is widely known that the Lebanese society of the past was closer to the collectivistic, *gemeinschaft* type of societies than the individualistic, *gesellschaft* type. By exhibiting a high level of individualism, the Lebanese youth are dispelling the myth that depicts Lebanon as a collective, communal society where an individual's freedom is tremendously constrained by his/her social group.

While no claim is made that individualistic values would certainly translate into individualistic behavior, recent studies indicate that attitudes predict future behavior if attitudes and behaviors are measured at the same level of specificity.[2] Moreover, keen observers of college students attest to this shift from collectivism to individualism, and even from modern to postmodern attitudes and behavior.[3]

The low value of the index of authoritarianism reflects a normative change away from the enduring value of respect for and obedience of authority figures in the Lebanese society. Again, the data are consistent with personal observations and discussions with colleagues. Lebanese youths, much like their western counterparts, no longer espouse the once sacred value of obedience to the parents, the elderly, the teachers, let alone political leaders. Even children are now less respectful of authority figures than their older cohorts.

To be sure, not all students are equally individualistic or rebellious. Two factors seem important enough to create significant variations in the level of authoritarianism and individualism, namely, gender and the nature of academic setting. Contrary to conventional wisdom, young women are more individualistic and less obedient to authority than their male counterparts. If anything, this reflects a radical, yet silent transformation in social values and norms.

At the level of group affiliations, the nuclear family is the most important reference group to students, followed by the extended family. In the pre-war period, Melikian and Diab also found the family (with no distinction between nuclear and extended) to comprise the most important social group with which students are affiliated. Religion is less important to them than the family and the local community, but sectarianism continues to maintain strong roots in their thoughts and practices, as other previous studies have also shown. The most significant determinant of the intensity of sectarianism is the extent of religiosity. A more religious person, regardless of his/her sect, tends to exhibit more intense sectarian feelings and attitudes than a less religious person. Still, family ranks first, irrespective of one's religion or degree of religiosity.

As for political norms, there is a powerful ideological trend toward Lebanese nationalism, which now predominates over the other ideologies among all social groups. Before the war, pan-Arabism attracted a substantial proportion of the youth, particularly Muslims. After the war, this ideology lost its wide support even among Muslims, a loss not necessarily due solely to war. A similar ideological trend toward local as opposed to pan-Arab nationalism has been observed in most other Arab countries.

Despite the dramatic rise in Lebanese nationalism among students, not one of the local political leaders has won the status of a student role model. On the contrary, students are pessimistic about their future in Lebanon because of the current economic conditions and the reign of corruption in the public administration.

In light of these main findings, it is important to highlight their implications, particularly for policy making in Lebanon. In addition, specific suggestions are made for fostering social justice, peace, and democracy.

Individual Values

On most of the individual values examined, Lebanese students exhibit characteristics of modern, or postmodern, rather than traditional society. They are probably as individualistic as postmodern Western people, increasingly seeking self-actualization and self-fulfillment. Their attitude toward authority is similar to what is now observed in Western Europe and Northern America where there is a decline in the acceptance of authority at home and the work place.[4] Equalitarianism is a cherished value to most students. Despite their long-term exposure to political turmoil and life-threatening situations, Lebanese students have maintained an impressive internal control over their lives.

The dominance of individualism as opposed to collectivism at the personal level has important implications for Lebanon at the societal level. Collectivist societies, some social scientists argue, are more vulnerable than the individualist society to ethnic cleansing and sectarian conflicts.[5] Hence, the rise of individualism among Lebanese students may contribute to reducing the intensity of sectarian loyalties among them.

Espousal of equalitarianism and detestation of authority are consistent with students' deep-rooted conviction in social equality and democracy. Some scholars assert that the declining respect for authority and the rising emphasis on self-actualization, participation, and self-expression are "conducive to democratization in authoritarian societies."[6] These values are also cherished by most if not all Lebanese. This explains why recurrent attempts by some politicians to detour Lebanon away from the path of political democracy are met with popular dissent from various religious communities.

The two strongest predictors of most individual values are university, or type of academic setting, and sex. The academic settings contrasted are those of AUB and LU; the former is an elitist, private institution for middle and upper-class clients, while the latter is a public, less competitive institution for lower and lower middle classes. For LU students to come out more individualistic and equalitarian than AUB students is a healthy sign for the future of democracy and modernization in Lebanon. When the masses of citizens begin to act according to the values of individualism and equalitarianism more strongly than the upper class elite, the political state has but a little margin to maneuver away from the path of democracy and modernity. In other words, the popular support for democracy deters the state from adopting autocratic practices even when it so desires.

It is quite inspiring to find female students more enthusiastic than male students about social equality and individualism and less supportive of blind obedience to established authorities. Since women have historically been the oppressed, subordinated, and subdued sex, their new challenging attitudes and values are salient signs of imminent social change. Moreover, these emerging values reflect changes in the nature of social relations within the nuclear family, as elaborated in the next section. Although Lebanese adult women have not yet played a powerful visible role in social change, time might prove that their young daughters are capable of creating a new image for the Lebanese woman.

Group Affiliations

The persistence of family allegiance is a testimony of a stable hierarchy of group affiliations among college students, a sign of stability in that aspect of the normative structure of the Lebanese society. Nevertheless, the continuous trend toward nucleation of the family signals an important change in other aspects of the normative pattern and social structure as well. Other societies have passed through a similar phase of social change that ended in a radical rupture with their past. Although the pace of change in Lebanon may not be rapid enough to generate an impending revolution in family patterns, the extent and nature of change should not be underestimated.

Survey findings clearly reveal significant alterations in relations within the family. One can neither assume a Lebanese father to be a "patriarch," nor a mother to be totally dependent and passive. Young adults are acting assertively by challenging the authority of their parents, albeit without severing the social bond that connects them. Talking back to parents in a loud voice is a grave violation of the norm of reverence for parents. Independence of mind regarding career choice and personal relations reflects the students' firm will to behave in ways that are novel to parents and that also allow for the students to gain independence from authority figures in the family. Males and females alike show this propensity, but the attitude and behavior of girls is particularly disconcerting to parents. Parents react with fuming anger when their daughters challenge and defy their orders. This demonstrates the gravity of the change the parents are experiencing with their children. Daughters are no longer docile, dependent, hapless creatures who cower under the pressure of their fathers, older brothers, or prospective husbands.

Underlying all this transformation are the "modern" Lebanese fathers who have nurtured more self-reliant, confident, and individualistic children than their own "traditional" fathers had done. Many modern fathers were not aware of the consequences of their new style of upbringing, and they may live to regret it. Reflecting on his experience with the youth generation, the famous Egyptian writer, Towfiq al-Hakim, wrote:

> In the past, our fathers used to impose their will on us. At present, we find our children intent on imposing their will on us. Is it likely we are the generation that has no will?!... We gave it up to our fathers in reverence and to our children in encouragement?![7]

As a result of the effects of parents' modern styles of childrearing, along with students' exposure to Western models and ideals and the individualizing impact of a protracted civil strife, a new type of relationship has emerged within the Lebanese nuclear family. Democratic relations are gaining ground at the expense of the old conservative patriarchal forms. This ensuing phenomenon has far-reaching implications for the Lebanese society. Since the family is the most fundamental basis of society and politics, any radical change in it is bound to generate change in all other aspects of life. A dramatic shift in the nature of authority and gender relations within the Lebanese family would create a ripple effect that would spread through other social institutions such as educational organizations, business establishments, and the political system. Consequently, this effect would shake the very foundations of Lebanon. The entire inter-locking system of sectarianism, parochial politics, authoritarianism, and patronage would break down, paving the way for a new, more liberal, Western-style alternative.

To be sure, such a scenario is unlikely to materialize in the coming few years since the pace of change does not seem to be that rapid. There are staunch, powerful opponents at every societal level. Inside the family, males will not give up their long held prerogatives without a fierce fight. Politicians, who are overwhelmingly male, would utilize every available mean to thwart such an eventuality. Religious sectarian organizations and their influence, which permeate various social institutions, would also resist with full force. In addition, religiosity seems to be capable of derailing people from the path of family democratization and gender equality since it predicates on rigid, conservative, and sectarian interpretations of religion. A more rational and modern interpretation of religion, particularly Islam, would further strengthen the modernizing trend. Given that, it is not surprising that advocates of fundamentalist, rigid views of religion are resorting to all sorts of tactics, from bribery to intimidation, in order to prevent dissemination of alternative modern views.

Despite all these obstacles, the trend toward nucleation and democratization of the family is robust and irreversible. It is a slow but sure path, yielding in the long-term a profound transformation in the very structure of social organization and the normative system. In order to facilitate this change, the guardians of patriarchy in the family— fathers, older brothers, and other male elders—should be educated to accommodate the legitimate and just concerns of their female "dependents" in order to minimize the adverse effects of confrontation between them. Public agencies, like the Ministry of Culture and Higher Education, NGOs, and particularly the media, can play a very helpful role to that effect.

Political Norms

For college students to find no role models among local politicians is not unique to the case of Lebanon. Annual surveys of American Freshman students have also documented a diminishing interest in politics over time. A common reason for the students' stance is their declining trust in politicians after a multitude of scandals that smeared the reputation of once prominent leaders, such as the late President Nixon and the current President Clinton. Most American youths have reacted to political scandals and problems with apathy. "Whatever you do, it won't make a big difference," said some of them. In reaction to major national issues, many have shown resignation. This outcome "both results from and furthers a more general erosion of American political life."[8]

As for Lebanon, anecdotes of nepotism, corruption, and abuse of authority did not spare any politician. Whether or not these anecdotes are true is not as important as the fact that people perceive them to be so.

After all, individuals tend to hurt each other over misconceptions. And since students' responses clearly underscore their belief that Lebanese politicians in general are not trustworthy, the political implications of these perceptions (or misperceptions) must be examined.

Students' dissatisfaction with politicians, as well as the entire regime, leads them to one of two likely outcomes:

- A sense of apathy and feeling of impotence in the face of domineering external forces. There is evidence that many students have developed these feelings. Some of them pursue personal fortunes and pleasures instead of active involvement in public issues, leading to more selfish attitudes and the eventual loss of the sense of community. Other members of this group may get so alienated from the political system that they may turn into social misfits engaging in drugs, alcoholism, and other forms of social deviance.[9]

- Defiance and rebellion. The goal of this category of students is to change what is perceived as "corrupt," "unfair," or "oppressive" in the political status quo. The reported willingness of the large majority of LU students to take action should be of concern to policy makers and scholars alike. What is now vague, fuzzy, and unspecified can eventually turn into an intelligent, crystallized plan of revolutionary action that would explode in the face of the ruling elite. History proves the great likelihood of such a scenario in the event that economic conditions deteriorate and political life slides into excessive authoritarianism and restrictive freedoms. Lebanese youth can be active "agents" of change that would, in Giddens' terms, "produce" new social realities and power structures. Postwar achievements of the government—from the huge reconstruction projects and rehabilitation of public services and physical structures to economic stability and the normalization of life—could evaporate into thin air under the strikes of angry and daring young rebels.

At the root of much of Lebanon's chronic ailments is sectarian politics, which remains alive and well after fifteen years of strife and seven years of peace. Halim Barakat once wrote:

> Confessionalism and familism constitute the most pervasive, diffuse, and enduring loyalties undermining nationalism in Lebanon.[10]

The enduring struggle among sects and their leaders for primacy does not bode well for the stability and sustained development in a postwar society. It is high time for the government to capitalize on the supportive voices of the youth that call for the abolition of sectarianism from politics. This would be in line with the amended Article 95 of the constitution, which calls for the establishment of a national council to be entrusted with that task. Forming this council is a necessary prelude for ending sectarianism in public administration.

To achieve this goal, much thought has to be put into the concrete measures that the government ought to take. One such measure is to involve college students in promoting and implementing the process of elimination of sectarian practices from public agencies. For example, a student representative could serve on the aforementioned national council. Students could be asked to appear on television shows to voice their opinions on the matter, volunteer to hang posters and distribute leaflets urging the Lebanese for support. They can be very effective in counterbalancing the social forces that would resist that process. Their involvement, however, requires a Lebanese regime that is seriously committed and strongly motivated to the elimination of sectarianism. So far, there are no clear signs of such a commitment on the part of the present government.

For the first time in Lebanon's history, a majority of young Lebanese from various sects unequivocally subscribes to Lebanese nationalism. The political elite should capitalize on this ideological transformation. It is a hopeful sign for integrating the various Lebanese communities, provided that the other divisive forces are neutralized or weakened. Educational institutions play a very effective role.

At the school level, much has to be done in the area of the curriculum, particularly the content and approach to social studies. For example, the curriculum should address ethnic and cultural diversity, learning about other religions, respect for human rights, citizenship education, and the tolerance for different viewpoints. Simplified courses on conflict resolution are also recommended for students at all levels, including pre-school. Many schools operating in different cultures have come to realize the merits of incorporating these courses in their curricula. Some schools in the United States use peer mediation to settle disputes among students. Outdoor activities should become part and parcel of the school curriculum. During these activities, students often learn more from each other during interpersonal communication over an extended period of time than they do from books and classroom teachers. The Lebanese youths from different religions, districts, and social classes should be offered the opportunity to interact with one another in an open, tolerant setting.[11]

At the university level, it would be useful to introduce courses on conflict analysis and resolution. Such courses, which include both theoretical and applied components, serve to teach students basic skills in listening to one another, empathizing, and tolerating their differences. In addition, the students would learn to resolve their interpersonal and inter-communal problems peacefully and in ways acceptable to all disputants. In the United States, some universities have created new bodies on campuses, such as mediation centers, in order to mediate disputes.

Besides the curriculum, several measures can be taken to foster religious and political tolerance, mutual understanding among communities, and eventually, national integration. For example, community centers can serve as magnets that attract the young and the old through specific social activities; they can become a desirable meeting place to discuss common problems in a non-threatening environment. Another useful measure is the summer camps that some NGOs have organized since the end of the war. The camps proved useful in reducing tension and misconceptions among the youths that belonged to formerly antagonistic communities. Seasonal camps, however, are less effective than regular ones, particularly if they are part of the school curriculum.

If this experiment succeeds, the foundations for future coexistence and national integration would be more robust than if powerful forces imposed coexistence, be they internal or external. On the basis of the study findings, such measures, if properly prepared and supported by all concerned parties—parents, schools, communities, universities, government, media, and NGOs—are bound to be successful and productive. A coordinating committee for the various groups, institutions, and individuals who are interested in pursuing this goal would be in order.

Beyond these findings, an urgent plea is made for a perceptive understanding and dialogue between figures of authority in politics and society and Lebanon's youth. There are problems of miscommunication and lack of communication between young people and authority representatives such as parents, teachers, college administrators, and members of parliament and cabinet. Initiating dialogue cannot but be beneficial to both parties even if it proceeds on a bumpy road. Conversely, the lack of communication may result in dire consequences on the entire society.

One possible forum for involving the youth in public activities is to have their elected representatives sit on higher national councils. The long awaited Economic Social Council is one example. Lebanon has several other councils that provide advice to the government on a diversity of issues. It would be useful for members of these councils to hear the opinions of the future generation if they honestly believe in the significance of the youth's role in society. This step would serve the dual purpose of national reconciliation and democratization much better if adopted as part of a larger plan to widen political participation in the country.

So far, this study shows that students are only complaining and expressing anger and resentment toward what they perceive as wrong and unfair in the political system. If their voices are not heard, the youth might not stay idle. Once a radical core of students emerges and begins to mobilize the mass of students for subversive action against the symbols of political authority, the entire nation could slide back into a quagmire of violence and extreme politics.

Conclusion: A Silent Revolution

Through the eyes of college students, one visualizes the normative structure of the Lebanese society in its continuity and change. The political attitudes and norms of students reflect, to a great extent, those of the larger society. Ideologically, the prevalence of Lebanese nationalism over Arab nationalism, Syrian nationalism, and Islamism among students indicates a similar change in other segments of the population. Their emphasis on security as a priority task for cabinets in postwar Lebanon resonates well with a long-standing demand for security among the Lebanese. In detesting corruption in the government and declining to elevate any of the local politicians to the revered status of a national leader, students speak the language of the masses. The students' deep sense of angst about their future in Lebanon underscores the bleak assessment of the shrinking middle class for their economic well being in light of the growing chasm between the rich and the poor.

Students have painted inter-sectarian relations objectively and vividly, producing a realistic political map of coalitions and antagonistic fronts that religious sects have forged.   Sadly, this map reveals the continuity of sectarian politics as a major divisive force in Lebanon. The sway of sectarianism over the Lebanese is not challenged by the postwar regime, which lacks a sincere, uncompromising policy to end all forms of sectarian practices in political life. The youth, however, overwhelmingly support the abolition of sectarianism despite the presence of sectarian loyalties among many of them. A genuinely secular government can capitalize on this position of the youth to implement its declared intention to end sectarian politics except at the level of the three top positions (President, Prime Minister, and House Speaker).

Still, regardless of the government's position, voluntary associations and highly motivated citizens are active "agents" who can make a difference in reducing sectarian feelings and behavior in a variety of ways. Among other tactics, a concerted action by NGOs, op-eds in newspapers, radio bulletins, television shows, and speeches by notables and respected members of the various communities are helpful. In other countries, the experience of these groups and individuals as part of civil society demonstrates the strong likelihood of success. Three crucial elements for their success are determination, perseverance, and the coordination of their activities.

A silent normative transformation in individual values is taking place, notably, in the direction of individualism, equalitarianism, and gender equality But a more far-reaching revolutionary change that is seeping silently through society is the rise in democratic practices within the Lebanese nuclear family. The nuclear family form is rapidly gaining ground at the expense of the traditional extended form. Democratization of relations within the family is winning over authoritarianism.

As the number of Lebanese women in higher education rises and their participation in the labor force increases, it would be almost impossible for men to bottle them again inside their homes, much like a genie out of the bottle. The international movement toward gender equality and empowerment of women is sweeping the world. Once it gains momentum in Lebanon, women would demand to be heard, and forces of opposition would then have to yield.

APPENDIX A

TABLES

Table A1: **Analysis of Variance**: Individualism by Sex, University, Major Father's Occupation, Mother's Education, and Parents' Place of Residence.

Source of Variation	Sum of Squares	DF	Mean Square	F	Sig. of F
Main Effects	59.590	10	5.959	8.130	.000
Sex	16.627	1	16.627	22.685	.000
University	13.365	1	13.365	18.234	.000
Major	10.957	3	3.652	4.983	.002
Father's Occupation	5.562	2	2.781	3.794	.023
Mother's Education	8.338	2	4.169	5.687	.003
Parents' Residence	4.741	1	4.741	6.468	.011
Explained	59.590	10	5.959	8.130	.000
Residual	952.127	1299	.773		
Total	**1011.717**	**1309**	**.773**		

Table A2: Analysis of Variance: Authoritarianism by Sex, University, Major, Parents' Place of Residence

Source of Variation	Sum of Squares	DF	Mean Square	F	Sig. of F
Main Effects	49.606	14	3.543	5.53	.000
Sex	14.010	1	14.010	21.864	.000
University	10.671	1	10.671	16.655	.000
Major	13.004	3	4.335	6.765	.000
Parents' Residence	11.921	9	1.325	2.067	.029
Explained	49.606	14	3.543	5.530	.000
Residual	970.726	1515	.641		
Total	**1020.333**	**1529**	**.667**		

Table A3: Logistic Regression of Equalitarianism on University, Sex, and
Mother's Education

Model Chi-Square		Chi-Square	DF	Significance			
		143.241	3	.000			
		Variables in the Equation					
Variable	B	S.E.	Wald	DF	Sig.	R	Exp (B)
Mother's Education	-.2155	.0930	5.3712	1	.0205	-.0457	.8062
Sex	-.4476	.0657	46.3641	1	.0000	-.1658	.6361
University	.5103	.0741	47.4037	1	.0000	.1677	1.6657
Constant	1.7692	.1953	82.0524	1	.0000		

Table A4: Analysis of Variance: Internal Control Scale by University and
Father's Occupation

Source of Variation	Sum of Squares	DF	Mean Square	F	Sig. of F
Main Effects	27.785	3	9.262	10.775	.000
University	17.491	1	17.491	20.350	.000
Father's Occupation	10.294	2	5.147	5.988	.003
Explained	27.785	3	9.262	10.775	.000
Residual	1154.348	1343	.860		
Total	**1182.134**	**1346**	**.878**		

Table A5: Analysis of Variance: Fatalism by Father's Occupation, Sex, University, and Major.

Source of Variation	Sum of Squares	DF	Mean Square	F	Sig. of F
Main Effects	194.2728	10	19.427	15.105	.000
Father's Occupation	28.782	1	28.782	22.379	.000
Sex	53.377	1	53.377	41.502	.000
University	60.028	1	60.028	46.674	.000
Major	21.166	3	7.055	5.486	.001
Religiosity	30.917	4	7.729	6.010	.000
Explained	194.270	10	19.427	15.105	.000
Residual	1660.384	1291	1.286		
Total	**1854.654**	**1301**	**1.426**		

Table A6: Logistic Regression of Asabiya Value on University and Religiosity

	Chi-Square	DF	Significance				
Model Chi-Square	18.364	2	.0001				
	Variables in the Equation						
Variable	**B**	**S.E.**	**Wald**	**DF**	**Sig.**	**R**	**Exp (B)**
University Lebanese	.1327	.0540	6.0291	1	.0141	.0426	1.1419
Religiosity	.2213	.0828	7.1368	1	.0076	.0481	1.2477
Constant	-.9536	.2233	18.2339	1	.0000		

Table A7: Logistic Regression of Dislike for Group Work on Major, Religiosity University, and Individualism

Model Chi-Square	Chi-Square 55.594		DF 4	Significance .0000			
	Variables in the Equation						
Variable	B	S.E.	Wald	DF	Sig.	R	Exp (B)
Major Humanities & Soc. Sc.	-2140	.0705	9.2220	1	.0024	-.0699	.8073
Religiosity	-.2450	.0986	6.1784	1	.0129	-.0532	.7827
University Lebanese	-.2318	.0715	10.5032	1	.0012	-.0758	.7931
Individualism	.3908	.0826	22.3780	1	.0000	.1174	1.4781
Constant	1.7145	.3265	27.5681	1	.0000		

Table A8: **Analysis of Variance**: Strength of Female Stereotypes by Sex, Religiosity, Sect, and Social Class

Source of Variation	Sum of Squares	DF	Mean Square	F	Sig. of F
Main Effects	232.426	9	25.714	8.652	.000
Sect	64.499	4	16.125	5.426	.000
Religiosity	122.337	3	40.779	13.721	.000
Father's Occupation	12.231	1	12.231	4.115	.043
Sex	32.359	1	32.359	10.888	.001
Explained	231.426	9	25.714	8.652	.00
Residual	1016.435	342	2.972		
Total	**1247.861**	**351**	**3.555**		

Table A9: Multiple Classification Analysis: Strength of Female Stereotypes by Sex, Religiosity, Sect, and Social Class

Variable	Category	N	Unadjusted		Adjusted for Independents	
			Dev'n	Eta	Dev'n	Beta
Sex	1 Male	200	.22		.27	
	2 Female	152	-.30		-.36	
				.14		.17
Religiosity	0 Non Believer	27	-1.70		-1.76	
	1 Believer & No Practice	158	-.23		-.24	
	2 Believer & Occasional Practice	62	.26		.43	
	3 Believer & Regular Practice	105	.62		.56	
				.32		.33
Sect	1 Maronite & Catholic	70	-.57		-.76	
	2 Orthodox	62	-.51		-.30	
	3 Sunni	122	.36		.26	
	4 Shiite	66	.52		.41	
	5 Druze	32	-.20		.40	
				.24		.24
Father's Occupation	1 Worker	92	.31		.19	
	2 All Other Occupations	260	-.11		-.07	
				.10		.06
	Multiple R	.431				
	Multiple R Squared	.185				

Grand Mean=4.48

Table A10: Logistic Regression of Attitude Toward Civil Marriage on Religiosity, Political Orientation, Sex, and Sect: AUB 1993

Model Chi-Square	Chi-Square	df	Significance
	135.440	9	.0000

Variables in the Equation

Variable	B	S.E.	Wald	df	Sig	R	Exp(B)
Political Orientation			3.4219	2	.1807	.0000	
Lebanese	.0965	.1528	.3914	1	.5315	.0000	1.1003
Arab Nationalism	.3028	.1754	2.9817	1	.0842	.0321	1.3536
Religiosity	.8531	.0991	74.1801	1	.0000	.2753	2.3469
Sect			7.7926	5	.1680	.0000	
Maronite	-.0111	.2163	.0026	1	.9590	.0000	.9889
Catholic	.0727	.2443	.0885	1	.7661	.0000	1.0754
Orthodox	.3367	2.188	2.3692	1	.1238	.0197	1.4004
Sunni	-.3681	.1592	5.3432	1	.0208	-0.592	.6921
Shiite	-.2194	.1852	1.4035	1	.2361	.0000	.8030
Sex: Male	.1128	.0874	1.6647	1	.1970	.0000	1.1194
Constant	-1.5510	.2455	39.9182	1	.0000		

Note: "Islamism" is the excluded category from the categorial variable "political orientation,": "Druze" is the excluded category from the variable "sect," and "female" is the excluded category from the variable "sex."

Table A11: Multiple Classification Analysis: Sectarianism by Political Ideology and Religiosity, AUB 1993

Variable					
			Unadjusted		Adjusted for Independents
Category		N	Dev'n	Eta	Dev'n	Beta
Ideology	1 Lebanese Nationalism	510	-.04		-.02	
	2 Arab Nationalism	122	-.50		-3.9	
	3 Syrian Nationalism	20	-1.99		-1.34	
	4 Islamism	57	2.14	.37	1.49	.26
Religiosity	1 Believer & Regular Practice	228	1.05		.53	
	2 Believer & Occasional Practice	158	.08		.09	
	3 Believer & No Practice	271	-.62		-.50	
	4 Non-Believer	52	-1.58	.42	-1.30	.34
Multiple R Squared					.235	
Multiple R					.485	

Grand Mean=2.56

Note: Interaction between ideology and religiosity is not significant.

Table A12: AUB Students' Perceptions of Relations Among Confessional Groups in Lebanon, 1993

Which is Closest to Your Sect?	Student's Sect (%)					
	Maronite	Catholic	Orthodox	Sunni	Shiite	Druze
Maronite	-	31	13	2	3	6
Catholic	50	-	46	5	1	0
Orthodox	18	31	-	19	6	8
Sunni	8	10	14	-	71	14
Shiite	2	4	2	51	-	22
Druze	5	0	3	1	3	-
All Other Muslims	1	4	2	2	1	14
All Other Christians	4	2	2	2	3	5
All Sects	1	0	1	2	3	3
None is Close	7	8	4	9	6	24
Total %	100	100	100	100	100	100
Number of Students	100	50	112	269	145	63

Table A13: AUB Students' Perceptions of Relations Between Confessional Groups in Lebanon, 1993

| | Student's Sect (%) | | | | | |
Which is Closest to Your Sect?	Maronite	Catholic	Orthodox	Sunni	Shiite	Druze
Maronite	-	7	14	34	40	28
Catholic	0	-	4	1	0	0
Orthodox	0	5	-	2	2	0
Sunni	1	7	4	-	2	6
Shiite	39	33	29	6	-	13
Druze	28	24	25	31	37	-
All Other Muslims	6	0	5	0	0	2
All Other Christians	0	0	0	5	3	15
All Sects	9	2	2	5	5	13
None is Close	6	12	3	8	7	11
Total %	**100**	**100**	**100**	**100**	**100**	**100**
Number of Students	**92**	**45**	**105**	**238**	**131**	**53**

APPENDIX B

QUESTIONNAIRES

1993 AUB Survey

To begin with, please give us the following information about your personal and family background by circling the number that corresponds to your answer.

1. Sex: 1. Male   2. Female

2. Major: 1. Engineering/Architecture
                2. Medicine
                3. Nursing
                4. Health Sciences
                5. Agriculture/Nutrition
                6. Science (Arts & Sciences)
                7. Business/Economics
                8. Humanities & Social Sciences (SBS, History, PSPA,
                   Education, Philosophy)
                9. Literature & Languages (Arabic, English)

3. Place of parents' (or guardians) current residence:
                              1. In Lebanon   2. Abroad

If your answer is "**In Lebanon**", specify:

                Muhafazaa:_____;
                Qada: _____;
                City or village:_____;
                If city, specify Street or Quarter_____.

4. Do you live in the dorm ?   1. Yes   2. No

5. Were you ever displaced because of the war for more than 6 consecutive months?
        1. Yes   2. No

6. Over the past 5 years, did you stay abroad for more than 6 consecutive months?
        1. Yes   2. No

7. Specify the level of education and the occupation of each of your parents

	Education			Occupation
Primary	Intermediate	Secondary	University	(give details, like teacher in a primary school)
1	2	3	4	
Father				
Mother				

8. Do your parents belong to:
    1.   Same religion and sect
    2.   Same religion but different sects
    3.   Different religions and sects

9. Did you take courses or lectures in religion at school?
        1. Yes   2. No

10. IF YES, at which school level were these courses offered:
    1. Primary 2. Intermediary   3. Secondary   4. Two or more levels

11. Did the majority of the students at your primary school have the same religion?
        1. Yes   2. No

12. During the Lebanese war, many people had all sorts of difficulties and tragic experiences. Did you, a member of your immediate family, or a close friend experience any of the following?

Type of experience	you		family or friend	
	Yes	No	Yes	No
a. Death caused by war		X		
b. Injury/kidnapping				
c. Displacement				
d. Major property damage				

Now we would like you to think of the social groups you belong to. These groups affect our lives in various ways, and we may be proud of them.

13. Which of the following groups do you consider yourself most closely tied to:

    1.   Your immediate family (parents and siblings)
    2.   Your extended family (parents, siblings, and all other relatives)
    3.   Your religious sect
    4.   The geographic area you live in (city quarter, suburb, or village)
    5.   The place you were born or raised in
    6.   A certain political party or militia
    7.   Others, specify: _____

14. Which of the above groups (or other unmentioned groups) do you consider to be second and third in importance in your life?

    Second in importance:_____

    Third in importance : _____

15. How do you assess your ties to other members of your extended family:
    1. Very close and intimate with frequent visits and mutual assistance
    2. Somewhat close with occasional visits and mutual assistance
    3. Distant with no mutual assistance
    4. Others, specify: _____

16. Which of the religious sects do you consider to be closest to your sect (not necessarily to yourself)?

    _____

17. Which of the religious sects do you consider to be most distant from your sect (not necessarily from yourself)?

    _____

18. Do you prefer to get married to a person who belongs to your religious sect?
    1. Yes   2. No

19. Do you prefer to live in a neighborhood where most residents belong to your religious sect?
    1. Yes
    2. I don't care about the residents as long as the house is convenient
    3. I prefer neighborhoods that have a religious mix of people
    4. Others, specify:_____

20. Do you usually buy goods from shops that are owned by:
    1. People belonging to your sect
    2. People belonging to your religion, not necessarily the same sect

3. People belonging to your ethnic or nationality group (e.g. Armenian)
4. I shop in my neighborhood
5. I go to shops that offer reduced prices irrespective of other factors
6. Others, specify: _____

21. What is the religious sect of your best friend? _____

22. If your sect gets in conflict with members of another sect, will you support your sect without any question or reservation)
      1. Yes   2. No

23. From a religious viewpoint, do you consider yourself:
1. A believer who practices religious rituals such as praying, fasting....
2. A believer who does not practice religious rituals
3. A non-believer
4. Others, specify: _____

24. If you are a believer who practices religious rituals, how often do you practice these rituals:
1. Regularly
2. Occasionally
3. Very rarely

25. Name three leaders (political, military, religious, artists,...) that you prefer MOST (in order of preference):
1. _____
2. _____
3. _____

26. Name three leaders that you dislike MOST:
1. _____
2. _____
3. _____

27. What is your religious sect:
   1.   Maronite
   2.   Catholic
   3.   Orthodox
   4.   Other Christian
   5.   Sunni
   6.   Shiite
   7.   Druze
   8.   Other Muslim

28. Do you consider yourself to be:
   1.   Lebanese nationalist
   2.   Arab nationalist
   3.   Syrian nationalist
   4.   Islamic nationalist
   5.   Islamic transnationalist
   6.   Others, specify:_____

29. Do you wish to see any change in the current political system in
    Lebanon?
       1. Yes   2. No

30. IF YES, specify the changes you wish to see:_____

31. Do you think that the Hariri government will succeed where previous
    governments failed?
       1. Yes   2. No

32. Do you think that the Hariri government will be able to solve at least a
good part of :
                                          1. Yes   2. No
   a.   Lebanon's political problems
   b.   Lebanon's economic problems
   c.   Lebanon's social problems
   d.   Will complete implementation of Taif Accords

33. Do you think the Palestinians in Lebanon should be given the right to become Lebanese citizens, if they so wish?
      1. Yes   2. No

34. IF NO, why?

    _____

    _____

35. What categories of Palestinians did you have contact with? (you can circle more than one category)

  1. No previous contact
  2. Militia members
  3. Neighbors/classmates/work mates
  4. Kin
  5. Others, specify: _____

36. In your opinion, what are the <u>three</u> most important social issues that the Lebanese people must address (Rank them in order of importance, i.e., most important and least important)

_____ a. Inequality of opportunity among citizens
_____ b. Housing shortages and high rents
_____ c. Lack of proper medical care for the needy
_____ d. High tuition at schools
_____ e. Immortality and corruption in public and private sectors
_____ f. Violence and aggressivity among people
_____ g. Continuous cuts in electric power
_____ h. Shortage of water supply
_____ i. The system of garbage disposal
_____ j. Others, specify: _____

Please read each of the following statements, then specify whether you:
STONGLY AGREE (5)
AGREE (4)
DISAGREE (2)
STRONGLY DISAGREE (1) with each of them
Write the code of your answer (i.e., 5,4, 2, or 1) in the spaces provided

_____ 37. I believe that my sect can serve Lebanon better than any other sect.

_____ 38. My sect is superior to all other sects.

_____ 39. My sect is dispriveleged in the current political system

_____ 40. Lebanon should become a secular state (i.e. religious affiliation should not affect appointments in public positions).

_____ 41. Civil marriage should be instituted in Lebanon.

_____ 42. I am strongly attached to my family.

_____ 43. I am strongly attached to my sect.

_____ 44. One should live among people of his sect.

_____ 45. Non-Lebanese individuals, other than Palestinians, should be allowed to become Lebanese citizens, if they so wish.

1994 AUB Survey

First, we would like you to give us some background information about
yourself.

1. Sex: 1. Male   2. Female

2. Major:
    1. Engineering/Architecture
    2. Medicine
    3. Nursing
    4. Health Sciences
    5. Agriculture/Nutrition
    6. Science (Arts & Sciences)
    7. Business/Economics
    8. Humanities & Social Sciences (SBS, History, PSPA, Education, Philosophy)
    9. Literature & Languages (Arabic, English)

3. Class: 1. Freshman 2. Sophomore 3. Junior 4. Senior 5. Graduate

4. Place of parents' current residence:
     1. Abroad   2. In Lebanon 3. Parents Dead

If your answer is "**In Lebanon**", specify:
    Muhafazaa:_____;
    Qada: _____;
    City or village:_____;

5. If parents are alive, ask: Are your parents:
1. Living together 2. Divorced/Separated 3. One parent deceased 4. One parent away

6. If parents live together, ask: Do you live with your parents? 1. Yes   2. No

7. If not living together, ask: With whom do you live?
      1. Father   2. Mother   3.Relative 4. Other

8. Over the past 5 years, did you stay abroad for more than 2 consecutive years since you were 14 years old?
      1. Yes   2. No

9. Specify the level of education and the occupation of each of your parents

Education				Occupation
Primary	Intermediate	Secondary	University	(give details, like teacher in a primary school)
1	2	3	4	

Father

Mother

Now, we'd like to ask you about your relationship with your parents. As you may know, young people have different experiences with their parents.

10. How do you describe your relationship with each of your parents?
5. Very close 4. Close 3. Somewhat close 2. Not close   1. Distant 0. Parent dead
              -----father   ------mother

11. Who do you get along with better?
1. Your father 2. Mother   3. Both, no difference   4. Neither   0. Not applicable

12. What are the three most important issues of dispute with your parents (one or both)
    1.
    2.
    3.

13. In each of the statements below, specify how often that thing happens you.

Does it happen: 5. Always 4. Often 2. Seldom or 1. Never?

a- My parents get upset when I don't do my chores/duties after I've been told to   -----

b- My parents get upset when I stay out later than I'm allowed to   -----

c- My parents get upset when I don't do well in my courses   -----

d- My parents get upset when they discover that I have a boyfriend/girlfriend   -----

e- My parents get upset when I yell back at them   -----

f- My parents get upset when I don't help out after I'm asked to   -----

g- My parents get upset when I don't tell them where I'm going   -----

h- My parents get upset when I intentionally ignore them (both or either)   -----

i- I get upset when my parents don't let me go out when I want to   -----

j- I get upset when my parents don't tell me the truth   -----

k- I get upset when my parents interfere in my life outside the home   -----

l- I get upset when my parents treat me like a child   -----

m- I get upset when my parents scold me in front of my friends   -----

n- My father is very authoritarian and domineering   -----

o- My mother/father is very overprotective   -----

14. When a conflict arises between you and your parents, how do you usually deal with it?

1.   Do you try to discuss the problem with them?
2.   Ignore them for a while then apologize
3.   Ignore the conflict and continue interacting with them as usual

4. Disobey them and do what you want without letting them know
5. Make an effort to do what they want you to do
6. Parents try to discuss the problem, giving you their point of view
7. Parents ignore the conflict and continue interacting with you as
8. usual
9. Parents punish you in some ways like stopping the allowance, ...
10. Other, specify--

Questions 15-20 are **ONLY FOR GIRLS**

If mother works, ask 15-16

15. Do you approve of your mother's work outside the home? 1. Yes   2. No

16. Why? Would you elaborate.

17. Do you plan to work after you graduate?   1. Yes   2. No

18. Mothers influence their daughters in more than one aspect of their lives.
    Kindly rank the following 7 aspects of life from 1 to 7 in order of
    importance, 7 being the most important and 1 the least.
----- Choosing a major profession
----- Choosing friends, fiance
----- Financial areas (buying, selling, borrowing things/money)
----- Religious beliefs, rituals, and social values (like honesty, pride
      freedom)
----- Appearance (what to dress, makeover, etiquette)
   -- Future plans (marriage, choice of residence, travel, where to work)
 --- Other, specify ---

19. Which of these activities do you do with your mother? (can check more
    than one)
    1. Shopping
    2. Cooking
    3. Other housework (cleaning, decoration....)

4.   Social visits
5.   Going out to restaurants, movies, theaters, clubs, or exercising together
6.   Travel
7.   Other, specify ------------------------------

20. When you talk to your mother, what topics do you discuss? (can check more than one)

1.   School work
2.   Your relations with family members
3.   Your relations with friends (boys & girls)
4.   Financial matters (need for money, what to buy, sell, borrow)
5.   Religious beliefs, social values (like honesty, freedom), politics
6.   Your appearance (what to dress, makeover, etiquette)
7.   Future plans (marriage, choice of residence, travel, where to work)
8.   Other, specify _____

TO ALL STUDENTS: Following are some questions about the role of women in Lebanese society, as you perceive them.

21. In your family, who decides on each of the following matters? Write the answer code
    1. Father 2. Mother 3. Both 4. Other relative 5. Nonrelative 6. Me
    7.Collective decision

a. Which schools children go to _____
b. Which person you may marry _____
c. Selection of food for your meals _____
d. Whether or not to buy a car/furniture/land and details of the purchase _____
e. Selection of family doctor, lawyer _____
f. Selection of family lawyer _____
g. Selection of bank _____
h. Type of house the family will live in (number of rooms, area, village) _____

In this section, we'd like to get your views on a number of important social issues.
Do you: (1) agree or (2) disagree with each of the following statements?

_____ 22. A housewife should have access to her husband's account either by having a joint account or a separate account for herself.

_____ 23. I prefer to work under a male boss.

_____24. Women are inferior to men.

_____25. Some jobs are inappropriate for women.
If Agree, name 3 such jobs: (1) _____ (2)_____ (3)_____

___26. Women should be allowed to work outside the home irrespective of their marital status (i.e., being single, married, divorced, or widowed).

___27. Mothers with young children should not be allowed to work outside the home

___28. Wives should have an equal say to their husbands in all family matters.

___29. The most important social role for a woman is to be a housewife-mother.

___30. One rarely gets married to a boyfriend/girlfriend.

___31. Premarital sex in our society should be allowed for both boys and girls.

___32. A girl should remain a virgin until marriage.

___33. Civil marriage should be instituted in Lebanon.

___34. The main goal of dating is to find the right marriage partner.

___35. Dating on AUB campus usually involves a sexual relation.

___36. Lebanese homosexuals (both gays and lesbians) are Lebanese citizens, and thus should be given the same rights of employment and college attendance as any other citizen.

If Agree, ask: 37. Would you have a homosexual as your close friend? 1. Yes 2. No.

Many people experience the things we'll tell you about in the statements below. On a scale from 0 to 10, please tell us how much that thing happens to you. Put 0 if you never have the experience and put 10 if it is always happening to you. If it happens sometimes, but not all of the time, put in one of the numbers between 0 and 10 to show how much.

0	1	2	3	4	5	6	7	8	9	10
(never)										(always)

___38. I find myself remembering bad things that happened to me over and over, even when don't want to think about them.

___39. When something reminds me of something bad that happened to me, I feel shaky, sweaty, nervous, and my heart beats really fast.

___40. I avoid doing things or being in situations that might remind me of something terrible that happened in the past.

___41. Sometimes I feel a bad event that happened in the past is happening again right now in the present, just as it did then.

___42. I feel very irritable and lose my temper.

___43. I have trouble getting to sleep or staying asleep.

Some claim that many AUB students use some form of drugs like hashish, cocaine, LSD, and crack. Our purpose is neither to identify nor incriminate the users, but to understand their behavior and beliefs.

___44. About how many drug users do you know or have you heard about?

___45. Why do you think these students are on drugs? (can check more than one answer)

1. Out of curiosity
2. Are bored with life, sick with daily routines
3. To drive away loneliness.
4. To seek pleasure, feel high.
5. To relieve stress/tension from personal/family problems.
6. To relate better to friends, be more sociable, likable,...
7. Other, specify _____

___46. Were you ever offered drugs?   1. Yes   2. No

___47. Do you think there is harm is taking drugs occasionally?
        1. Yes   2. No

___48. Do you think drugs should be legalized in Lebanon? 1. Yes 2. No

49. From a religious viewpoint, do you consider yourself:
       1. A believer who practices religious rituals such as praying or fasting
       2. A believer who does not practice religious rituals
       3. A non-believer
       4. Others, specify: _____

50. If you are a believer who practices religious rituals, how often do you practice these rituals:
       1. Regularly
       2. Occasionally
       3. Very rarely

51. What is your religious sect?
    1. Maronite
    2. Catholic
    3. Orthodox
    4. Other Christian
    5. Sunni
    6. Shiite
    7. Druze
    10. Other Muslim

52. Finally we'd like to know how you rate the performance of the Hariri government to date.

Is it: 5. Excellent   4.Very good   3. Average   2. Bad   1. Very bad?

1996 AUB & LU Surveys

<u>Common Questions</u>

To begin with, please give us the following information about your personal and family background by circling the number that corresponds to your answer.

1. Sex: 1. Male   2. Female

2. Major:
1.   Engineering/Architecture
2.   Medicine
3.   Nursing
4.   Health Sciences
5.   Agriculture/Nutrition
6.   Science (Arts & Sciences)
7.   Business/Economics
8.   Humanities & Social Sciences (SBS, History, P
9.   Education, Philosophy)
10. Literature & Languages (Arabic, English)

3. Place of parents' (or guardians) current residence:
Abroad 1. Beirut city 2. Suburbs of Beirut 3. Other Mount Lebanon
4. Saida 5. Other South Lebanon 6. Tripoli   7. Other North Lebanon 8. Zahle or Baalbak 9. Other Beqa'

 4. Over the past 10 years, did you stay abroad for at least one year?
          1. Yes   2. No

5. Specify the level of education and the occupation of each of your parents

Education				Occupation
Primary	Intermediate	Secondary	University	(give details, like teacher in a primary school)
1	2	3	4	
Father				
Mother				

Now we would like you to think of the social groups you belong to. These groups affect our lives in various ways, and we may be proud of them.

6. Which of the following groups do you consider yourself most closely tied to:

Your immediate family (parents and siblings)
Your extended family (parents, siblings, and all other relatives)
Your religious sect
The geographic area you live in (city quarter, suburb, or village)
The place you were born or raised in
A certain political party or militia
Others, specify: _____

7. Which of the above groups (or other unmentioned groups) do you consider to be second and third in importance in your life?

Second in importance:_____

_____

Third in importance : _____

_____

Do you **agree (A) or disagree (D)** with each of the following statements:

___8. My life is usually determined by my own actions.

___9. I have found that what is going to happen will happen.

___10. When I make plans, I am almost certain to make them work.

___11. It's not always wise for me to plan too far ahead because many things turn out to be a matter of good or bad fortune.

___12. A person should always be the master of his own fate.

___13. A man must make his own decisions, uninfluenced by the opinions of others.

___14. I'd rather have a room to myself than a shared house.

___15. I usually prefer to work alone than be part of a team.

___16. I can pretty much determine what will happen in my life.

___17. When I get what I want, it is usually because I worked hard for it.

___18. When I get what I want, it's usually because I'm lucky.

___19. To a great extent, my life is controlled by accidental happenings.

___20. A man can learn better by striking out boldly on his own than he can by following the advice of others.

___21. In a small group, there should be no real leaders- everyone should have an equal say.

___22. Disobeying an order is one thing you can't excuse.

____23. In any organization, if you lay down a rule, it must be obeyed and enforced.

____24. I rebel against an authority when I believe it is unjust.

____25. When talking to people in Lebanon, one should pay attention to the style of the expressions more than their content.

____26. People in Lebanon are less moved by what you say than by how you say it.

____27. One must preserve appearances when in the company of others, whether friends or enemies.

____28. One must not hide one's troubles and problems from friends.

____29. It's all right to lie in order to save one's face.

____30. I like to work with my hands.

____31. I never fix things that break down even when I know how to fix them. I always ask someone to do that.

____32. Manual work is inferior to mental work even if it pays better.

____33. I always think of what people will say about my actions and behavior.

____34. I don't feel guilty if I do something wrong without being noticed by anyone.

____35. I'll always side with my brother against my cousin and with my cousin against a non-relative.

___36. I admire the man who uses all the shortcuts to achieve his goal without any exertion.

___37. Whoever works hard will achieve his goals in life.

___38. Before I act on something, I always ask myself: What will people say.

39. How important is religion in your life?
    5. Very important 4. Important 3. Neutral 2. Not important
                   1. Not important at all.

40. How often do you attend religious services?
    1. Regularly   2. Occasionally   1. Never

41. What is your religious sect?
    1. Maronite
    2. Catholic
    3. Orthodox
    4. Other Christian
    5. Sunni
    6. Shiite
    7. Druze
    10. Other

Questions To LU Students Only

42. Do you listen to news bulletins:
    1. Daily 2. Several times a week   3. Once a week or less 4. Never

43. Do you read newspapers:
    1. Daily 2. Several times a week   3. Once a week or less 4. Never

Now we'd like to ask you about your opinion regarding the current situation in Lebanon.

44. Specify in the order of importance (write "1" for the most important, "3" for the least important) three obligations the Lebanese government has towards citizens:

____ Security
____ Job opportunities
____ Social justice
____ Freedom of opinion and expression
____ Other, specify

45. Specify in the order of importance (write "1" for the most important, "3" for the least important) three main personal traits which a political leader must have:
___ Intelligence
___ Equality in dealing with people
___ Education
___ Fulfilling people's desires
___ Heading a political party
___ Honesty
___ Strong personality
___ Credibility

46. Do you find among politicians any role model? 1. Yes   2. No

    Why did you say so?_____

47. Name in the order of importance (write "1" for the most important, "3" for the least important) three political leaders you like.

48. Name in the order of importance (write "1" for the most important, "3" for the least important) three political leaders you hate.

49. Do you feel that you have a secure future in Lebanon? 1. Yes   2. No
    Why did you say so?_____

50. Does the government's performance make you fell secure about your future in Lebanon? 1. Yes 2. No
Why did you say so?_____

51. Do the policies of this government, in your opinion, express the youth's ambitions?
1.Yes 2. No
Why did you say so?_____

52. Do you ever come up with ideas about changing your present life conditions?
1. Yes 2. No
How? Elaborate_____

53. Do you prefer to work: 1. In Lebanon or 2. Abroad
Why did you say so?_____

54. Do you accept to take part in changing the current situation?
1. Yes 2. No
Why did you say so?_____

NOTES

---

1. Introduction

[1] The beginning of a poem by al-Akhtal al-Saghir, which was later composed into a song by The Flaifel brothers. For many years, this song was popular among the Lebanese youth. At elementary school in the 1960s, we used to sing it in music classes and at national ceremonies.

[2] For further reading on the role of students in social upheaval and radical change, see, for example, Frederich Engels, *Germany: Revolution and Counter-Revolution*, trans. L. Krieger, (New York: International Publishers, 1937); Jurgen Habermas, *Toward a Rational Society: Student Protest, Science, and Politics*, trans. Jeremy J. Shapiro, (Boston: Beacon Press, 1970); David E. Apter, ed., *Ideology and Discontent*, (New York: The Free Press, 1964), particularly the editor's introduction, pp. 28-30. For relevant work on Lebanon, see Halim Barakat, *Lebanon in Strife: Student Preludes to the Civil War*, (Austin, Texas: University of Texas Press, 1977).

[3] Apter, *Ideology and Discontent*, p. 28.

[4] See note 1.

[5] Noted examples are: Bashir Jemayyel, Amin Jemayyel, Elias Hobeiqa, Samir Ja'ja', and Anwar Fatayri. Both Amin and Bashir Jemayyel were leaders in the *Kataib* (also known as Phalangists) student organization when they were college students. Amin became a prominent member of the *Kataib* political party, while Bashir headed the Lebanese Forces, the once-dominant para-military organization that placed all the Christian Maronite militias under its umbrella. Bashir was elected president of Lebanon under the Israeli bayonets, but was assassinated before assuming office. His brother Amin, through parliamentary elections, succeeded him. Elias Hobeiqa and Samir Ja'ja' began their political activity in the *Kataib* student organization, then joined the Lebanese Forces. Hobeiqa succeeded Bashir Jemayyel as Chief when the latter assumed the presidency, but was soon

overthrown by Ja'ja' and forced out of the Christian-controlled areas. Ja'ja' then became Chief of the Lebanese Forces until they were banned and he was incarcerated in 1994.   Anwar Fatayri, a Druze, was one of the prominent leaders of the so-called "national" student movement before the civil war.   He was a member of the Progressive Socialist Party, a largely-Druze party that participated in the civil war through its para-military wing.   Fatayri played both political and military roles.

[6] For example, Marwan Hamadeh, a former student leader and a key member of the largely-Druze Progressive Socialist Party, has served as cabinet member in several cabinets since 1990 and is presently a member of parliament.   Muhammad Abdul-Hamid Beydoun is a member of parliament and of the leading committee of the Shiite movement *Amal*.   He is a former cabinet member and student leader in the Shiite organization of *Amal* during the civil war.   Elias Hobeiqa, a former student leader and militia chief (see note 5), has been a member of both cabinet and parliament since the end of the war.   Other noted field officers in the para-military organizations now occupy top positions in various public agencies.

[7] Estimation by author based on data from the 1996 Survey of Housing and Population that was conducted by the Lebanese government. The United Nations Fund for Population Activities provided technical support and funds for the survey.

[8] The age group 10-14 represents 10.6% of the total population in 1996, while the age groups 15-19 and 20-24 represent 10.1% and 9.7% respectively.

[9] One such plan aims at retraining government employees.

[10] Talcott Parsons, *The Social System*, (New York: Free Press, 1951).

[11] Ibid., p. 92.

[12] Jurgen Habermas, *The Theory of Communicative Action, Vol. One: Reason and Rationalization of Society*, (London: Heinemann, 1984), p. 124.

[13] One reading of Max Weber's classical work *The Protestant Ethic and the Spirit of Capitalism* indicates his cultural deterministic view.

[14] For details, see Jurgen Habermas, *The Theory of Communicative Action, Vol. Two: The Critique of Functionalist Reason*, (London: Heinemann, 1987).

[15] Anthony Giddens, *The Consequences of Modernity*, (Cambridge: Polity Press, 1990).

[16] For details, see chapter 2.

[17] Barakat, *Lebanon in Strife*.

[18] Levon H. Melikian and Lutfy N. Diab, "Stability and Change in Group Affiliations of University Students in the Arab Middle East, " *Journal of Social Psychology* 93 (1974): 13-21.

[19] Nafhat Nasr and Monte Palmer, "Alienation and Political Participation in Lebanon," *International Journal of Middle East Studies* 8 (1977): 493-516.

[20] Theodor Hanf, "Le Comportement Politique des Etudiants Libanais," *Travaux et Jours* 46 (Jan-March, 1973):5-52.

2. Values, Norms, and Change: A Sociological Perspective

[1] Immanuel Wallerstein, "Social Science and the Quest for a Just Society," American Journal of Sociology 102, no.5 (March): 1255.

[2] For more details, see Norman T. Feather, ed., *Expectations and Actions: Expectancy Value Models in Psychology* (Hillsdale, N.J.: Lawrence Erlbaum Associates, 1982).

[3] For details, see Seymour Epstein, "Values From The Perspective Of Cognitive-Experiential Self-Theory," *Social And Moral Values: Individual And Social Perspectives*, ed. Nancy Eisenberg, Janusz Reykowski, and Ervin Staub (Hillsdale, NJ: Lawrence Erlbaum Associates Publishers, 1989), p. 4.

[4] See Leonard H. Chusmir, Christine S. Koberg, and John Mills, "Male-Female Differences In The Association Of Managerial Style And Personal Values," *Journal of Social Psychology* 129, no. 1 (Feb. 1989): 65-78.

[5] For more details, read Talcott Parsons and Edward A. Shils, "Values, Motives, And Systems Of Action," *Toward A General Theory of Action*, ed. Talcott Parsons and Edward A. Shils (New York: Harper and Row, 1951).

[6] As cited in Anthony Giddens, *Politics, Sociology and Social Theory* (Stanford, CA: Stanford University Press, 1995), p. 288.

[7] Clyde Kluckhohn, "Values And Value Orientations In The Theory Of Action," *Toward A General Theory of Action*, ed. Talcott Parsons and Edward A. Shils (New York: Harper and Row, 1951), p. 395.

[8] Parsons and Shils, op.cit.

[9] Peter Ester et al., eds., *The Individualizing Society: Value Change In Europe And North America* (Tilburg, the Netherlands: Tilburg University Press, 1993), p. 22.

[10] Ibid., p. 22.

[11] Milton Rokeach, *The Nature of Human Values* (New York: The Free Press, 1973), p. 5.

[12] Robin M. Williams, Jr., "Change And Stability In Values And Value Systems: A Sociological Perspective," *Understanding Human Values, Individual And Societal*, ed. Milton Rokeach (New York: The Free Press, 1979), p. 16.

[13] Ibid., p. 16.

[14] Robert Nisbet and Robert G. Perrin, *The Social Bond*, 2d ed. (New York: Alfred A. Knopf, 1977), p. 43.

[15] For more details, see Abdullatif Muhammad Khalifa, *Irtiqa' al-Qiyam* (Hierarchy of Values), (Kuwait: National Council for Culture, Art, and Literature, 1992), chapter 10.

[16] Rokeach, *Nature of Human Values*.

[17] See for example, Feather, *Expectations and Actions*; Rokeach, *Nature of Human Values*; Williams, "Change and Stability;" Chusmir et al., "Male-Female Differences;" D.M. Mayton, S.J. Ball-Rokeach, J. Sandra, and W.E. Loges, "Human Values And Social Issues: An Introduction," *Journal of Social Issues* 50, no. 4 (winter 1994): 1-8.

[18] Adapted from John Scott, *Sociological Theory: Contemporary Debates* (Brookfield, Vermont: Edward Elgar Publishing Company, 1995), p. 67. Scott's illustration is based on: Talcott Parsons, *The Social System* (New York: Free Press, 1951), p. 37.

[19] Ibid., p. 66.

[20] Ibid., p. 21.

[21] Robert F. Meier, "Norms And The Study Of Deviance: A Proposed Research Strategy," *Deviant Behavior: Readings in the Sociology of Norm Violations*, ed. Clifton D. Bryant (New York: Hemisphere Publishing Corporation, 1990), pp. 128-148.

[22] William J. Goode, *The Celebration of Heroes* (Berkeley, CA: University of California Press, 1978), p. 10.

[23] Nisbet and Perrin, *Social Bond*, p.195.

[24] Ronald L. Akers, *Deviant Behavior: A Social Learning Perspective*, 2d ed. (Belmont, CA: Wadsworth, 1977), p. 7.

[25] Clifton D. Bryant, "The Social Context," *Deviant Behavior: Readings in the Sociology of Norm Violations*, op.cit., pp. 3-20.

[26] See, for instance, George Homans, *Social Behavior. Its Elementary Forms* (New York: Harcourt, Brace and World, 1961).

[27] As cited in John Scott, *Sociological Theory: Contemporary Debates* (Brookfield, Vermont: Edward Elgar Publishing Company, 1995), p. 37.

[28] Derek Layder, *Understanding Social Theory* (London: Sage publications, 1994), p. 22.

[29] As cited in Scott, *Sociological Theory*, p. 92.

[30] Jurgen Habermas, *The Theory of Communicative Action, Vol. One: Reason and Rationalization of Society* (London: Heinemann, 1984), p. 124.

[31] Jurgen Habermas, *Toward a Rational Society: Student Protest, Science, and Politics*, trans. Jeremy J. Shapiro, (Boston: Beacon Press, 1970), pp. 91-2.

[32] Meier, "Norms and the Study of Deviance."

[33] Most of the listed variations were indicated by Halim Barakat in his book *The Arab World: Society, Culture, and State* (Berkeley, CA: University of California Press, 1993), p. 190.

[34] For details, see Abdulrahman Ibn Khaldun, *The Muqaddima: an Introduction to History*, trans. Franz Rosenthal (Princeton, N.J.: Princeton University Press, 1967).

[35] According to Habermas' reading of Parsons. For details, see Jurgen Habermas, *Toward a Rational Society,* pp.91-94.

[36] For details, see any text on sociological theory such as L. Coser, *Masters of Sociological Thought*, 2d ed. (New York: Harcourt, Brace, Jovanovitch, 1977); Robert Nisbet, *Sociological Tradition* (New York: Basic Books, 1966); G. Ritzer, *Frontiers of Social Theory: the New Syntheses* (New York: Columbia University Press, 1990).

[37] Examples of relevant norms are: consumerism, self-actualization, and self-indulgence. Chapter 4 deals with the latter two under the heading "Individualism."

[38] For further reading on the modern world system, see Immanuel Wallerstein, *The Modern World System,* 3 vols. (San Diego: Academic Press, 1974-1988).

[39] Anthony Giddens, *Sociology* (Cambridge: Polity Press, 1989), chapter 16.

[40] See Mike Featherstone, *Global Culture: Nationalism, Globalization, and Modernity* (Newbury Park, CAL: Sage, 1990).

[41] Anthony Giddens, *New Rules of Sociological Method* (London: Hutchinson, 1976).

[42] See L. Althusser and E. Balibar, *Reading Capital* (London: New Left Books, 1970).

[43] For more details, see Layder, *Understanding Social Theory*, p.2.

[44] For example, George Herbert Mead and Herbert Blumer, both symbolic interactionists, Parsons the leading functionalist, and Althusser, a structural Marxist.

[45] Anthony Giddens, *The Constitution of Society* (Cambridge: Polity Press, 1984).

[46] Layder, *Understanding Social Theory*, p. 142.

[47] For more details, see Jeffrey C. Alexander and Steven Seidman, eds., *Culture and Society: Contemporary Debates* (Cambridge: Cambridge University Press, 1990), pp. 1-27.

[48] Karl Marx and Frederich Engels, *Selected Works* (London: Lawrence and Wishart, 1968), p. 96.

[49] This is also the viewpoint of Layder, *Understanding Social Theory*, pp. 143-144.

[50] Jurgen Habermas, *The Theory of Communicative Action, Vol. Two: The Critique of Functionalist Reason* (London: Heinemann, 1987), p. 192.

[51] This is also the viewpoint of Layder, *Understanding Social Theory*, p. 205.

[52] For details, see Habermas, *Theory of Communicative Action, Vol. Two.*

[53] Layder, *Understanding Social Theory*, p. 202.

[54] This is also the opinion of Ronald Inglehart which is elaborated in his book *Modernization and Postmodernization: Cultural, Economic, and Political Change in 43 Societies* (Princeton, NJ: Princeton University Press, 1997).

[55] This approach of "historical specificity" was advocated and employed by several scholars. For example, see Craig Calhoun, "Culture, History, and the Problem of Specificity in Social Theory," *Postmodernism and Social Theory: The Debate over General Theory*, ed. Steven Seidman and David Wagner (Cambridge, MA: Basil Blackwell, 1992). Halim Barakat used this approach in his discussion of Arab value orientations that appeared in *The Arab World*.

[56] See for example K. Deaux and B. Major, "Putting gender into context: an interactive model of gender-related behavior," *Psychological Review*, 94 (1987): 369-389.

[57] Susan E. Cross and Hazel Rose Markus, "Gender in Thought, Belief, and Action: A Cognitive Approach," in *The Psychology of Gender*, eds. Anne E. Beall and Robert J. Sternberg (New York: Guilford Press, 1993), p. 59.

[58] According to gender identity theory as explained in: Florence L. Geis, "Self-fulfilling Prophecies: A Social Psychological View of Gender," in Beall and Sternberg, *Psychology of Gender*, pp. 9-55.

[59] Cross and Markus, op.cit.

[60] Ibid., p. 60.

[61] K. Deaux and L.L. Lewis, "The structure of gender stereotypes: interrelationships among components and gender label," *Journal of Personality and Social Psychology,* 46 (1984): 991-1004.

[62] J.E. Williams and D.L. Best, *Measuring Sex Stereotypes: A Thirty Nation Study* (Beverly Hills, CA: Sage, 1982).

[63] Geis, "Self-fulfilling Prophecies," p. 15, cites several studies that provide supportive evidence.

[64] For citations of relevant studies, see ibid., pp. 18-19.

[65] Judith Lorber, "Gender," in *Encyclopedia of Sociology,* eds. Edgar F. Borgatta

and Marie L. Borgatta (New York: Macmillan, 1992), 2:749.
[66] See Talcott Parsons and Robert F. Bales, *Family, Socialization and Interaction Process* (New York: Free Press, 1955).
[67] Examples of studies are cited in Geis, "Self-fulfilling Prophecies," p. 25.

3. Research Review and Study Methodology

[1] Robert Merton, *On Theoretical Sociology: Five Essays, Old and New* (New York, Free Press, 1967), p. 4.
[2] See for example Doug Coupland, *Generation X* (New York: St. Martin's Press, 1991); *Shampoo Planet* (New York: Pocket Books, 1993).
[3] Daniel Bell, "Modernism, Postmodernism, and the Decline of Moral Order," *Culture and Society: Contemporary Debates*, ed. Jeffrey C. Alexander and Steven Seidman (Cambridge, MA: Cambridge University press, 1990), pp. 319-329.
[4] For more details, see Linda J. Sax, Alex W. Astin, William S. Korn, and Kathryn M. Mahoney, *The American Freshman: National Norms for Fall 1995* (Los Angeles, CAL: UCLA, 1995).
[5] Richard Easterlin and Eileen Crimmins, "Private Materialism, Personal Self-Fulfillment, Family Life, And Public Interest: The Nature, Effects, And Causes Of Recent Changes In The Values Of American Youth," *Public Opinion Quarterly* 55, no. 4 (winter 1991): 499-533.
[6] T. Kasser, R. M. Ryan, M. Zax, and A. J. Sameroff, "The Relations Of Maternal And Social Environments To Late Adolescents Materialistic And Prosocial Values," *Developmental Psychology* 31, No. 6 (Nov. 1995): 907-914.
[7] G. M. Rose, A. Shoham, L. R. Kahle, and R. Batra, "Social Values, Conformity, and Dress," *Journal of Applied Social Psychology* 24, No. 17 (Sept. 1994): 1501-1519.
[8] See note 4 of chapter 2.
[9] Several publications resulted from this survey such as Stephen Harding, David Phillips, and Michael Fogarty, *Contrasting Values in Western Europe: Unity, Diversity, and Change* (London: MacMillan, 1986).
[10] For details, see Peter Ester et al, *The Individualizing Society: Value Change in Europe and North America* (Tilburg, the Netherlands: Tilburg University Press, 1993).
[11] For details, read Ronald Inglehart, *Modernization and Postmodernization: Cultural, Economic, and Political Change in 43 Societies* (Princeton, NJ: Princeton University Press, 1997).

[12] For example, see Morroe Berger, *The Arab World Today* (Garden City, NY: Doubleday, 1962); Lois Beck and Nikkie Keddie, eds., *Women in the Muslim World* (Cambridge, MA: Harvard University Press, 1978); Dale Eickelman, *The Middle East: An Anthropological Approach* (Englewood Cliffs, NJ: Prentice-Hall, 1981); Peter Mansfield, *The Arabs*, (New York: Penguin, 1985); Leila Ahmed, *Women and Gender in Islam* (New Haven: Yale University Press, 1992); Halim Barakat, *The Arab world: Society, Culture, and State* (Berkeley: California University Press, 1992).

[13] For example, see Leonard Binder, ed., *Politics in Lebanon* (NY: Wiley, 1966); Fuad Khuri, *Tribe and State in Bahrain* (Chicago: Chicago University Press, 1980); Sherifa Zuhur, *Revealing Reveiling: Islamist Gender Ideology in Contemporary Egypt* (Albany, NY: State University of New York Press, 1992).

[14] For example, see Fuad Khuri, *From Village to Suburb* (Chicago: Chicago University Press, 1975); Elizabeth and Robert Fernea, *The Arab World: Personal Encounters* (Garden City, NY: Anchor Press/Doubleday, 1985).

[15] For examples of studies on the Arab world in general, see Sonia Hamady, *Temperament and Character of the Arabs* (NY: Twayne Publishers, 1960); Raphael Patai, *The Arab Mind*, rev. ed. (NY: Scribner, 1983); Hisham Sharabi, *Neopatriarchy: A Theory of Distorted Change in Arab Society* (NY: Oxford University Press, 1988). For examples of studies in Arab countries, particularly from a psychological perspective, see A.M. Khalifa, *Irtiqa' al-Qiyan* (Hierarchy of Values) (Kuwait: National Council for Culture, Art, and Literature, 1992).

[16] For example, see Halim Barakat, , *Lebanon in Strife: Student Preludes to the Civil War* (Austin, Texas: University of Texas Press, 1977); Zuhayr Hatab and Abbas Makki, *al-Sulta al-Abawiyya Washshabab* (Patriarchy and the youth), (Beirut: Ma'had al-Inma' al-Arabi, 1981); Hilal Khashan, *Inside the Lebanese Confessional Mind* (Lanham, MD: University Press of America, 1992); Nafhat Nasr and Monte Palmer, "Alienation and Political Participation in Lebanon," *International Journal of Middle East Studies* 8 (1977): 493-516.

[17] For example, see Fuad Khuri, *From Village to Suburb*; Samir Khalaf, *Reclaiming Beirut* (Beirut: Dar Annahar, 1993); Samir Khalaf and Philip Khoury, eds., *Recovering Beirut: Urban Design and Post-War Reconstruction,* (Leiden: Brill, 1993).

[18] Levon Melikian, "Themes in the Personality of Arab Youth," unpublished manuscript (Beirut: American University of Beirut, n.d.).

[19] Louise H. Kidder , *Selltiz, Wrightman and Cook's Research Methods in Social Relations*, 4th ed., (New York: Holt, Rinehart and Winston, 1981), p.261.

[20] Melikian, 196?, op.cit., p. 61.

[21] Ibid., p. 17.

[22] Ibid.

[23] Levon H. Melikian and Lutfy N. Diab, "Stability and Change in Group Affiliations of University Students in the Arab Middle East," *Journal of Social Psychology* 93 (1974): 13-21.

[24] One illustration of the forced choice question is the following:
"If to show your loyalty to your nation: (a) You were forced to give up your religion permanently, both in private and in public, or, (b) You were forced to give up your family and never see them again. Which would you choose? (a)_____ (b) _____ "
The corresponding rank-order question that I have used is:
"Which of the following groups do you consider yourself most closely tied to:
    1.   Your immediate family (parents and siblings)
    2.   Your extended family (parents, siblings, and all other relatives)
    3.   Your religious sect
    4.   The geographic area you live in (city quarter, suburb, or village)
    5.   The place you were born or raised in
    6.   A certain political party or militia
    7.   Others, specify: _____
Which of the above groups (or other unmentioned groups) do you consider to be second and third in importance in your life?
    Second in importance:_____
    Third in importance : _____ "

[25] Theodor Hanf, "Le Comportement Politique des Etudiants Libanais," *Travaux et Jours* 46 (Jan-March, 1973): 5-52.

[26] Nasr and Palmer, "Alienation and Political Participation."

[27] Barakat, *Lebanon in Strife*.

[28] Ibid., p.56.

[29] Khashan, *Inside the Lebanese Confessional Mind*.

[30] For further details, see chapter 7.

[31] Hilal Khashan, "The Political Values of Lebanese Maronite College Students," *Journal of Conflict Resolution*, vol. 34, no.4 (December 1990):723.

[32] Adnan al-Amin and Muhammad Faour, *University Students in Lebanon: Background and Attitudes* (Beirut: Lebanese Association for Educational Sciences, 1998).

[33] For example, see Samir Khalaf, *Reclaiming Beirut*.

[34] For example, see Theodore Hanf, *Coexistence in Wartime Lebanon* (London: Centre for Lebanese Studies, 1993).

[35] For more details, see Earl Babbie, *The Practice of Social Research*, 7th ed., (New York: Wadsworth, 1995), pp. 173-175.

[36] H. Barakat, *Lebanon in Strife*, table 3.3, p. 45.

[37] Ibid., p.44.

4. Stability and Change in Social Structure

[1] Iliya Harik, "Rethinking Civil Society: Pluralism in the Arab World," *Journal of Democracy*, vol. 5, no. 3 (July 1994): 56.

[2] The source is the 1996 survey of housing and population which was co-sponsored by the Lebanese Ministry of Social Affairs and UNFPA.

[3] Figures refer to national data from the *Enquete Sur La Population Actif Au Liban, Novembre 1970*, and the 1996 survey of housing and population, both conducted by government agencies.

[4] The 1971 data are from the 1971 national fertility survey, the results of which appeared in Lebanon Family Planning Association, *Al-Usra fi Lubnan* (The Family in Lebanon), 2 vols. (Beirut: Lebanon Family Planning Association, 1974). The 1996 data are from the 1996 Maternal and Child Health Survey of Lebanon that was conducted by the Ministry of Social Affairs in Lebanon.

[5] See Economist Intelligence Unit, *Country Profile: Lebanon, 1996-97* (London: Economist Intelligence Unit, 1997), p. 10.

[6] Ibid.

[7] The survey was conducted by the Central Directorate of Statistics, a public agency.

[8] See Economist Intelligence Unit, *Country Profile*, p.10

[9] Michael C. Hudson, *The Precarious Republic: Political Modernization in Lebanon*, A Westview Encore Edition, (Boulder, CO: Westview Press, 1985), p.6.

[10] See Robert A. Dahl, *Democracy and Its Critics* (New Haven, Conn.: Yale University Press, 1989), pp. 108-131. A good summary of the works of David Truman and Robert Dahl, two authorities on American democracy and pluralism, is given by Ronald Kahn in *Survey of Social Science: Government and Politics Series*, ed. Frank N. Magill (Englewood Cliffs, NJ: Salem Press), 4:1402-1403. Furthermore, the relevance of democratic requirements to other Arab countries is examined in Muhammad Faour, *The Arab World After Desert Storm* (Washington, D.C.: United States Institute of Peace, 1993), chapter 3.

[11] Emile Durkheim, *The Division of Labor in Society* (Glencoe, Ill.: Free Press, 1964), p. 28.

[12] Philippe Schmitter, "Society," in National Research Council, *The Transition to Democracy: Proceedings of a Workshop* (Washington, D.C.: National Academy Press, 1991), as cited in M. Faour, *Arab World*, p. 49.

[13] Iliya Harik, "Rethinking Civil Society," p. 51.

[14] For further details on the essential role of civil society in the democratization process, see Samuel Huntington, "Will More Countries Become Democratic?" in Samuel Huntington and Joseph Nye, Jr., eds., *Global Dilemmas* (Cambridge, Mass.: Harvard University Press, 1985), pp. 253-279. Iliya Harik, however, has doubts about the potential of civil society "as an engine of democratization." Instead, he calls for privatization of cultural and social organizations and considers the presence of multiple organizations in politics as "favorable to democracy." (ibid., p. 56).

[15] One poignant example is given in the section on economy.

[16] The secular parties that have shrunk to a handful of members are the Lebanese Communist Party and other smaller communist and socialist parties that were active until the early 1980s. The Syrian Social Nationalist Party is the main party that was weakened immensely after the withdrawal of many members and the inaction of many disillusioned others.

[17] For details on the election mechanism and nature of factions and blocs that existed in prewar Lebanon, read Hudson, *The Precarious Republic*, chapter 6, and Salibi, *A House of Many Mansions: The History of Lebanon Reconsidered* (London: I.B.Tauris & Co, 1988), chapter 10.

[18] Halim Barakat, *Lebanon in Strife: Student Preludes to the Civil War*, (Austin, Texas: University of Texas Press, 1977), p. 28.

[19] Ibid., p. 27.

[20] Ibid.

[21] See Kamal Salibi, *A House of Many Mansions*, chapter 12.

[22] Lebanese Parliament, House of Parliament, "The Lebanese Constitution with all Amendments" (Beirut, 1990), as cited and translated by Munir Bashshur, "Education and the Secular/Religious Debate: Illustrations from Lebanon," Working Paper no. 19 (Los Angeles, CA: G.E. von Grunbaum Center publications, 1992), p. 15. I introduced two minor changes: replaced the word "justly" with "fairly" and added an explanation between parentheses.

[23] Albert Hourani, *Syria and Lebanon* (London: Oxford University press, 1954), p. 64.

[24] Stephen Longrigg, *Syria and Lebanon Under the French Mandate* (London: Oxford University press, 1958), as cited in Bashshur, "Education & the Secular/Religious Debate," p. 8.

[25] The Shii Imam Shamsuddin is the highest authority in the recently established Islamic College. Patriarch Hazim of the Orthodox Christians heads the board of trustees of Balamand University. The Christian Maronite clergy run the Kaslik and Notre Dame universities. The Armenians run Haigazian College. Sunni Islamists run Annajah university in Tripoli, and the Sunni Mufti Qabbani and another Sunni Islamic group, known as al-Ahbash, are seeking government permission to open two new universities.

[26] For details, see Muhammad Faour, "The Demography of Lebanon: A Reappraisal," *Middle Eastern Studies*, vol. 27, no. 4 (October 1991).

[27] This view is also expressed by some academicians such as Samir Khalaf in: *Lebanon's Predicament* (New York: Columbia University Press, 1987), p. 19.

[28] Bashshur, "Education & the Secular/Religious Debate," p. 15.

[29] Max Weber, "Bureaucratic Authority," trans. Martin Black with Lance W. Garmer, in Wolf Heyderbrand, ed., Max Weber, *Sociological Writings* (New York: Continuum, 1994), p. 79.

[30] A noted example is Hariri's diplomatic success in winning the support of world leaders for Lebanon's case when Israel launched a military assault in 1996. Neither President Hrawi nor Speaker Berri has his personal stamina or international network of connections.

[31] This situation is expected to change after the election of Emile Lahud to the presidency of Lebanon.

[32] See William Harris, *Faces of Lebanon* (Princeton, NJ: Markus Wiener Publishers, 1997), p 297.

[33] As cited in Bashshur, "Education & the Secular/Religious Debate," p. 8

[34] No statistics on the religious composition of students are available. The rough comparisons made are based on Bashshur, "Education & the Secular/Religious Debate," pp. 17-18. However, the comparison of the proportions of Muslim and Christian students in American schools is based on personal observation (my two children are enrolled in the two main American schools).

[35] Ibid., pp. 20-22.

[36] Nemer Frayha, "Religious Conflict and the Role of Social Studies for Citizenship Education in the Lebanese Schools Between 1920 and 1983," (Ph.D. diss., Stanford University, June 1985), p. 346, as cited in Bashshur, "Education & the Secular/Religious Debate," p. 24.

37 For more details, read Halim Barakat, *The Arab world: Society, Culture, and State* (Berkeley: California University Press, 1992), Chapter 6.
38 Fuad Khuri, *Tents and Pyramids* (London: Saqi Books, 1990), p. 52 (computed by author from table 4).
39 For more details, read Hisham Sharabi, *Neopatriarchy: A Theory of Distorted Change in Arab Society* (NY: Oxford University Press, 1988), particularly pp. 2-8.
40 Ibid., p. 46.
41 Abdullah Laroui, *The Concept of the State* (Beirut: Dar al Haqiqa, 1973), p. 168 (Arabic), as cited in Sharabi, ibid., p. 132.
42 Sharabi, *Neopatriarchy*, p. 131.
43 Ibid.
44 Ibid.
45 Muhammad Faour, "Pan-Arab Cooperation after Desert Storm," *Austrian Journal of Development Studies* XI/4 (October 1995): 407-419. More details on the Arab order appear in Muhammad Faour, *The Arab World After Desert Storm* (Washington, D.C.: United states Institute of Peace, 1993).

5. Social Values: Between Tradition and Postmodernity

1 Ulrich Beck, *The Reinvention of Politics: Rethinking Modernity in the Global Social Order*, trans. Mark Ritter (Cambridge, MA: Polity Press, 1997), p. 96.
2 The original version of the questionnaire is placed in appendix B.
3 *Random House Compact Unabridged Dictionary*, special 2nd ed. (New York: Random House, 1996).
4 Lawrence Hazelrigg, "Individualism," in *Encyclopedia of Sociology*, eds. Edgar F. Borgatta and Marie L. Borgatta (New York: Macmillan, 1992), 2: 902.
5 Ibid., p. 905.
6 R.N. Bellah, R. Madsen, W.M. Sullivan, A. Swidler, and S.M. Tipton, *Individualism and Commitment in American Life: Readings on the Themes of Habits of the Heart* (New York: Harper and Row, 1988).
7 Harry C. Triandis, *Individualism and Collectivism* (Boulder, CO: Westview Press, 1995), p.6.
8 Ibid., p. 31, citing a survey of social scientists conducted by the author and a collaborator: C.H.Hui and H.C.Triandis, "Individualism and Collectivism: A Study of Cross-Cultural Researchers," *Journal of Cross-Cultural Psychology* 17 (1986):225-248.
9 These statements represent respectively questions 12, 13, and 20 of Questionnaire

3 in the appendix. They are taken from Robert F. Bales and Arthur S. Couch, "The Value Profile: A Factor Analytic Study of Value Statements," *Sociological Inquiry* 39 (winter 1969): 3-17.

[10] Peter Ester et al., eds., *The Individualizing Society: Value Change In Europe And North America* (Tilburg, the Netherlands: Tilburg University Press, 1993), p.214.

[11] This is one of the conclusions of interviews conducted by one of my graduate students with several women in senior positions in the Lebanese government.

[12] For details, see chapter 7, the section on sectarianism.

[13] Triandis, *Individualism and Collectivism*, pp. 62-63.

[14] *Random House Dictionary*, op.cit

[15] Ibid.

[16] For further reading on Adorno's work, see T.W. Adorn et al., *The Authoritarian Personality* (New York: Harper Brothers, 1950).

[17] These statements represent respectively questions 22, 23, and 24 of Questionnaire 3 in appendix B. The first two questions are taken from R.F. Bales and A.S. Couch, "The Value Profile". The third question was phrased by the author.

[18] *Random House Dictionary*, op.cit.

[19] This statement appears as questions 21 of Questionnaire 3 in the appendix. It is taken from R.F. Bales and A.S. Couch, "Value Profile." Since this individual value is measured in terms of one item, it is neither an index, nor does it tap the various meanings associated with the concept of equalitarianism.

[20] These statements represent respectively questions 8, 10, 16, and 17 of Questionnaire 3 in appendix B. They are drawn from Hanna Levinson, "Multidimensional Locus Of Control In Psychiatric Patients," *Journal of Consulting and Clinical Psychology* 41, 3 (1973):397-404.

[21] Halim Barakat, *The Arab World, Culture, and State* (Berkeley: California University Press, 1992), p. 194. In this book, Barakat provides a critical review of the works of several Western scholars such as Morroe Berger, G.E. Von Grunebaum, and R. Patai.

[22] These statements represent respectively questions 9, 11, 18, and 19 of Questionnaire 3 in appendix B. They are drawn from H. Levinson, ibid.

[23] This inference is obtained by comparing the "betas" in the multiple classification analysis table.

[24] More details on the characteristics of medical and health students were presented earlier in this chapter.

[25] These statements represent respectively questions 27, 28, and 29 of

Questionnaire 3 in the appendix. They are drawn from Raphael Patai, *The Arab Mind*, rev. ed. (New York: Scribner, 1976), p. 105.

[26] These statements represent respectively questions 14 and 15 of Questionnaire 3 in the appendix. The first one is a modified version of the statement "I'd rather have a mat of my own than a shared house," which is cited in Patai, op.cit., p. 110. The second is composed by the author to tap the same concept.

[27] These statements represent respectively questions 30, 31, and 32 of Questionnaire 3 in the appendix. They are based on ideas expressed by R. Patai, *Arab Mind*, p.113-116.

[28] These statements represent respectively questions 25 and 26 of Questionnaire 3 in the appendix. They are based on ideas expressed by H. Barakat, *Arab World, Culture and State*, p. 200.

[29] These statements represent respectively questions 33, 34, and 38 of Questionnaire 3 in appendix B. They are based on ideas expressed by R. Patai, *Arab Mind* and H. Barakat, *Arab World, Culture and State*.

[30] The mean value of the index of manual work is equal to 0.80 for LU students and 0.54 for AUB students. The difference of means is statistically significant at the .0001 level ($t=6.54$).

[31] The mean value of the index of face saving is equal to 1.48 for LU students and 1.65 for AUB students. The difference of means is statistically significant at the .0001 level ($t=3.87$).

6. Family Norms: Persistence and Change

[1] Surah 17:23-24 of the Koran, as cited in 'Abdullah Yusuf Ali, *The Meanings of the Holy Qur'an*, new ed. (Brentwood, MD: Amana Corporation, 1993).

[2] Sheldon Stryker, "Identity Theory," in *Encyclopedia of Sociology,* eds. Edgar F. Borgatta and Marie L. Borgatta (New York: Macmillan, 1992), 2: 873.

[3] See Levon H. Melikian and Lutfy N. Diab, "Group Affiliations of University Students in the Arab Middle East," *Journal of Social Psychology* 49 (1959): 145-159.

[4] The data were collected by Levon H. Melikian and Lutfy N. Diab. Findings of the earlier study were published in the article cited in the previous endnote. Findings of the later study appeared in: Levon H. Melikian and Lutfy N. Diab, "Stability and Change in Group Affiliations of University Students in the Arab Middle East," *Journal of Social Psychology* 93 (1974): 13-21.

[5] See Hisham Sharabi, *Neopatriarchy: A Theory of Distorted Change in Arab*

Society (NY: Oxford University Press, 1988).

[6] Melikian and Diab, "Group Affiliations."

[7] For more details, see Ali Zay'our, *The Psychoanalysis of the Arab Self* (Beirut: Dar Attali'ah, 1977), p. 34 (in Arabic), as translated by Sharabi, *Neopatriarchy*, p. 41.

[8] For example, Samir Khalaf in his book *Lebanon's Predicament* (New York: Columbia University Press, 1987), p. 119, states: "A Christian is first a Christian , a member of a given family, and from a specific region before he is a Lebanese."

[9] Surah 17:23-24 of the Koran, as cited in 'Abdullah Yusuf Ali, *The Meanings of the Holy Qur'an*, new ed. (Brentwood, MD: Amana Corporation, 1993).

[10] 1996 Survey of Housing and Population in Lebanon.

[11] The data on Lebanese adult women will be analyzed in a separate study.

[12] Bernice Lott and Diane Maluso, "The Social Learning of Gender," in *The Psychology of Gender*, eds. Anne E. Beall and Robert J. Sternberg (New York: Guilford Press, 1993), pp. 99-123.

[13] For details and empirical evidence, see the final report of the Arab Conference on the Implementation of the ICPD Plan of Action, UN-ESCWA, September 22-25, 1998.

[14] For details, see chapter 5.

[15] For more information about marriage contracts and *'isma*, see for example, Shaikh Ahmad Muhammad Assaf, *Al-Halal Wal Haram fi Al-Islam* (Permissiveness and Prohibition in Islam) (Beirut: Dar Ihya' al-'Ulum, 1983), pp. 148-149. In this book and others, it is claimed that a proud, decent man would not accept to sign a marriage contract that empowers his wife to initiate divorce.

7. Political Attitudes and Norms

[1] Elissa El Hashem, "Alwailu lahum min Ghadbat Asha'b" (Woe on them from the people's wrath), *Nahar Ashabab*: Hyde Park (Dec. 19, 1996): 25.

[2] Halim Barakat, *Lebanon in Strife: Student Preludes to the Civil War*, (Austin, Texas: University of Texas Press, 1977).

[3] Theodore Hanf, "Le Comportement Politique des Etudients Libanais," *Travaux et Jours* 46 (Jan-March, 1973): 5-52.

[4] Nafhat Nasr and Monte Palmer, "Alienation and Political Participation in Lebanon," *International Journal of Middle East Studies* 8 (1977): 493-516.

[5] Hilal Khashan, *Inside the Lebanese Confessional Mind* (Lanham, MD: University Press of America, 1992).

[6] Khashan (ibid.) asked the same question but did not present the detailed responses in his book. Instead, he examined the relation between the religious affiliation of the student and that of the preferred leader, which is also examined later in this chapter.

[7] Al-Amin and Faour in 1997 asked two separate questions about preferred leaders: one about local politicians and the other about international and regional leaders. In response to the first question, LU students (first and second branch combined) in the 1997 survey chose Najah Wakim as the most preferred local politician (14%) followed by Nasrallah and Aoun (each 11%). Among the favored international leaders, the Pope was most popular among LU students (26%), closely followed by President Assad of Syria (24%). President Chirac came third with 12% of the students selecting him as most preferred. These results are roughly consistent with the 1996 data despite the differences in the survey date and the question wording of the present data. Furthermore, it should be noted that the non-response rate for these questions in the 1997 survey was high: over 20% in both AUB and LU.

[8] In the 1997 survey of AUB students, Hariri was most popular (25%) followed by Wakim then deputy Nassib Lahhoud (12% and 11% respectively). At AUB, both the Pope and Assad were tied for the first place (20%), closely followed by President Chirac of France (18%).

[9] Wider exposure of AUB students to the international system of information is mainly due to their better knowledge of English, the language of the modern information super highway, their American academic training (since the U.S.A. is the most advanced nation in technology whose economic and information influence covers the entire globe), and their social network of wealthier, more educated sophisticated individuals.

[10] The 1997 survey had almost the same results: Hariri was most disliked by 30% of the students while Murr was disliked by 10%.

[11] In the 1997 survey, Murr was most disliked by 18% of the students while Hariri was most disliked by 13% of them.

[12] Khashan (*Inside the Lebanese Confessional Mind*) had the same general conclusion.

[13] For more details, see chapter 4, "Religion."

[14] For details on the religious distribution of the population of Lebanon, see Muhammad Faour, "The Demography of Lebanon: A Reappraisal," *Middle Eastern Studies* 27, no. 4 (December 1991).

[15] Hanf, "Compartement Politique," p. 26.

[16] Nasr and Palmer ("Alienation and Political Participation," p. 497) reported that

most students before the war at both AUB (78%) and LU (77%) desired radical change in Lebanese political institutions, with significant differences by social class (negative monotonic relationship) and religion (Shiite Muslims were most alienated while Maronite Christians were least alienated).

[17] By comparison, 86% of AUB students in 1971 stated: " There is a great deal of corruption and favoritism in the political administration in my country." (Halim Barakat, *Lebanon in Strife: Student Preludes to the Civil War* (Austin, Texas: University of Texas Press, 1977), p. 210.)

[18] Michele Deeb Fallah, "Almazra'a" (Fiefdom), *Nahar Ashabab*: Hyde Park (Oct. 8, 1996): 27.

[19] Rana Sh'aito, "Khatt Ahmar" (Red line),), *Nahar Ashabab*: Hyde Park (Oct. 29, 1996): 28.

[20] The percentages of Catholic, Orthodox, and Shiite students who assessed the performance of the government as bad or very bad were 16, 19, and 22 respectively. The variation of this score by sect is statistically significant at the .001 level (Chi Square=23.87, degrees of freedom—d.f.—equal 5).

[21] The conceptual link between gender and values is discussed in chapter 5 that focuses on the topic of individual values and norms where gender looms large.

[22] For details, see Muhammad Faour, *The Arab World After Desert Storm* (Washington, D.C.: United states Institute of Peace, 1993), chapter 4.

[23] According to Khashan (*Inside the Lebanese Confessional Mind*, p. 67), the majority of university students from all but two religious sects (Shiites with 20%, and Orthodox with 47%) expressed their determination "to support their sect unquestioningly" if a conflict arises between their sect and another sect. The highest proportion of supporters for one's own sect was reported by the Maronite and Druze students (73% and 75% respectively).

[24] According to Emile Durkheim, religion is a "unified system of beliefs and practices relative to sacred things... which unite into one single moral community." (*The Elementary Forms of Religious Life* (London: Allen, 1926), p. 61. Of the two components of religion, beliefs and rites, Durkheim regards the latter as more important for integration of society (see B.S. Turner, *Religion and Social Theory* (London: Sage, 1991), p. 47). Yet, both components are used in this study to measure religiosity. In the 1993 and 1994 surveys at AUB, religiosity included the following four categories: (1) a believer who practices religious rituals regularly, (2) a believer who practices religious rituals occasionally, (3) a believer who rarely practices religious rituals, and (4) a nonbeliever. The degree of religiosity is thus highest in category "1" and lowest in category "4" and the variable was treated as

continuous. In the 1996 surveys at AUB and LU, religiosity was measured in terms of two questions. The first question was: "How important is religion in your life? (5) Very important, (4) Important, (3) Neutral (2) Not Important (1) Not Important At All." The second question was: "How often do you attend religious services? (1) Regularly, (2) Occasionally, (3) Never." Both questions have been used repeatedly in studies on values. See for example Ann M. Beutel and Margaret Mooney Marini, "Gender and Values," *American Sociological Review* 60 (June 1995): 436-448.

[25] The nine items that make up the index of sectarianism are:

- I believe that my sect can serve Lebanon better than any other sect.
- My sect is superior to all other sects.
- I am strongly attached to my sect.
- One should live among people of his sect.
- Do you prefer to live in a neighborhood where most residents belong to your religious sect?
- Do you usually buy goods from shops that are owned by people belonging to your sect?
- If your sect gets in conflict with members of another sect, would you support your sect without question
    or reservation?
- Do you prefer to get married to a person who belongs to your religious sect?
- Those students who selected "religious sect" as the social group to which they are most closely tied (question 13 in the 1993 AUB questionnaire, appendix B), were assigned a score of 1, the others 0.

Students who answered yes to the first eight statements were assigned a score of 1, otherwise 0. The scores for all nine items were then added for each student. As a result, the index ranged from 0 to 8, where 0 means no sectarian loyalty and 8 means highest level of sectarianism.

[26] A number of studies are cited in Ann M. Beutel and Margaret Mooney Marini, "Gender and Values," *American Sociological Review* 60 (June 1995): 439.

[27] Ibid.

[28] A good yet brief overview of relevant literature is offered in Beutel and Marini, ibid., p. 437.

[29] For example, see Dorie Giles Williams, "Gender Differences in Interpersonal Relationships and Well-being," *Research in Sociology of Education and Socialization* 5 (1985): 230-267.

[30] For explanation of the statistical terms that appear in the tables and the technique of multiple classification analysis, the reader can refer to any relevant statistics

text. A good source on this method is Frank M. Andrews et al., *Multiple Classification Analysis*, 2nd ed. (AnnArbor, MI: University of Michigan, 1973).

8. Changing Norms: Implications and Suggestions

[1] Riad Solh is the first Prime Minister of Lebanon after its independence from France. He gave that statement on October 7, 1943 as part of a speech to the parliament to seek a vote of confidence for his cabinet.

[2] This statement is in accordance with a recent review of a large number of studies. For more details, see Stephen J. Kraus, "Attitudes and the Prediction of Behavior: A Meta-Analysis of the Empirical Literature," *Personality and Social Psychology Bulletin*, 21 (1, 1995): 58-75.

[3] This contention is based on informal discussions with colleagues who teach social sciences in different universities in Lebanon.

[4] For details, see Peter Ester et al., eds., *The Individualizing Society: Value Change In Europe And North America* (Tilburg, the Netherlands: Tilburg University Press, 1993), particularly pp.146-147.

[5] Harry C. Triandis, *Individualism and Collectivism* (Boulder, CO: Westview Press, 1995), pp. 179-180.

[6] Ronald Inglehart, *Modernization and Postmodernization: Cultural, Economic, and Political Change in 43 Societies* (Princeton, NJ: Princeton University Press, 1997), p. 43.

[7] Tawfiq al-Hakim, *Thowrat Ashabab: Qadiyat al-Qarn al-Wahid Wal'ishrin* (Youths' revolution: the issue of the twenty-first century) (Cairo: Adab bookshop, 1984), p. 37.

[8] Paul Rogat Loeb, *Generation at the Crossroads: Apathy and Action on the American Campus* (New Brunswick, N.J.: Rutgers University Press, 1994), p. 25.

[9] While no adequate statistics on the prevalence of deviant behavior on campuses or elsewhere in Lebanon exist, personal observations of students and conversations with colleagues from other universities assert their visible presence on various college campuses. As to empirical evidence from AUB, the responses of students to a couple of questions on drug use provide some insight into the scale of the problem. When AUB students in 1994 were asked: "Were you ever offered drugs?" Close to one-fifth of the students (28% of the males and 7% of the females) answered in the affirmative. A much larger percentage (46%) reported knowing drug users.

[10] Halim Barakat, *Lebanon in Strife: Student Preludes to the Civil War*, (Austin,

Texas: University of Texas Press, 1977), p. 33.

[11] A new curriculum will be in effect in the fall of 1998 but its full content was not available at the time of this writing. Furthermore, it will take few more years before one can assess the impact of the new curriculum on students' political and social norms.

BIBLIOGRAPHY

Adorno, T.W., E. Frenkel-Brunswick, D. Levinson, and R. Sanford. *The Authoritarian Personality*. New York: Harper Brothers, 1950.

Ahmed, Leila. *Women and Gender in Islam*. New Haven: Yale University Press, 1992.

Akers, Ronald L. *Deviant Behavior: A Social Learning Perspective*. 2d ed. Belmont, CA: Wadsworth, 1977.

al-Amin, Adnan, and Muhammad Faour. *University Students in Lebanon: Background and Attitudes*. Beirut: Lebanese Association for Educational Studies, 1998.

Alexander, Jeffrey C., and Steven Seidman, eds. *Culture and Society: Contemporary Debates*. Cambridge: Cambridge University Press, 1990.

al-Hakim, Tawfiq. *Thowrat Ashabab: Qadiyat al-Qarn al-Wahid Wal'ishrin* (Youths' Revolution: The Issue of the Twenty-First Century). Cairo: Adab bookshop, 1984.

Althusser, L., and E. Balibar. *Reading Capital*. London: New Left Books, 1970.

Andrews, Frank M., James N. Morgan, John A Sonquist, Laura Klem. *Multiple Classification Analysis*. 2nd ed. Ann Arbor, MI: University of Michigan, 1973.

Apter, David E., ed. *Ideology and Discontent*. New York: The Free Press, 1964.

Assaf, Shaikh Ahmad Muhammad. *Al-Halal Wal Haram fi Al-Islam* (Permissiveness and Prohibition in Islam). Beirut: Dar Ihya' al-'Ulum, 1983.

Babbie, Earl. *The Practice of Social Research*. 7th ed. New York: Wadsworth, 1995.

Bales, Robert F., and Arthur S Couch. "The Value Profile: A Factor Analytic Study of Value Statements." *Sociological Inquiry* 39 (winter 1969): 3-17.

Barakat, Halim *The Arab World: Society, Culture, and State.* Berkeley, CA: University of California Press, 1993.

———. *Lebanon in Strife: Student Preludes to the Civil War.* Austin, Texas: University of Texas Press, 1977.

Bashshur, Munir. *Education and the Secular/Religious Debate: Illustrations from Lebanon.* Working Paper No. 19. Los Angeles, CA: G.E. von Grunbaum Center publications, 1992.

Beck, Lois, and Nikkie Keddie, eds. *Women in the Muslim World.* Cambridge, MA: Harvard University Press, 1978.

Beck, Ulrich. *The Reinvention of Politics: Rethinking Modernity in the Global Social Order.* Trans. Mark Ritter. Cambridge, MA: Polity Press, 1997.

Bell, Daniel. "Modernism, Postmodernism, and the Decline of Moral Order." *Culture and Society: Contemporary Debates.* Ed. Jeffrey C. Alexander and Steven Seidman. Cambridge, MA: Cambridge University press, 1990.

Bellah, R.N., R. Madsen, W.M. Sullivan, A. Swidler, and S.M Tipton. *Individualism and Commitment in American Life: Readings on the Themes of Habits of the Heart.* New York: Harper and Row, 1988.

Berger, Morroe. *The Arab World Today.* Garden City, NY: Doubleday, 1962.

Beutel, Ann M., and Margaret Mooney Marini. "Gender and Values." *American Sociological Review* 60 (June 1995): 436-448.

Binder, Leonard. ed. *Politics in Lebanon* NY: Wiley, 1966.

Bryant, Clifton D. "The Social Context." *Deviant Behavior: Readings in the Sociology of Norm Violations.* Ed. Clifton D. Bryant. New York: Hemisphere Publishing Corporation, 1990.

Calhoun, Craig. "Culture, History, and the Problem of Specificity in Social Theory." In *Postmodernism and Social Theory: the Debate Over General Theory,* ed. Steven Seidman and David Wagner. Cambridge, MA: Basil Blackwell, 1992.

Coser, L. *Masters of Sociological Thought.* 2d ed. New York: Harcourt, Brace, Jovanovitch, 1977.

Coupland, Doug. *Generation X.* New York: St. Martin's Press, 1991.

_____. *Shampoo Planet.* New York: Pocket Books, 1993.

Cross, Susan E., and Hazel Rose Markus. "Gender in Thought, Belief, and Action: A Cognitive Approach." In *The Psychology of Gender,* ed. Anne E. Beall and Robert J. Sternberg. New York: Guilford Press, 1993.

Dahl, Robert A. *Democracy and Its Critics.* New Haven, Conn.: Yale University Press, 1989.

Deaux, K., and L.L Lewis. "The Structure of Gender Stereotypes: Inter-relationships Among Components and Gender Label." *Journal of Personality and Social Psychology,* 46 (1984): 991-1004.

_____, and B. Major. "Putting Gender into Context: An Interactive Model of Gender-Related Behavior." *Psychological Review,* 94 (1987): 369-389.

Durkheim, Emile. *The Division of Labor in Society.* Glencoe, Ill: Free Press, 1964.

_____. *The Elementary Forms of Religious Life.* London: Allen, 1926.

Easterlin, Richard, and Eileen Crimmins. "Private Materialism, Personal Self-Fulfillment, Family Life, and Public Interest: The Nature, Effects, and Causes of Recent Changes in the Values of American Youth." *Public Opinion Quarterly* 55, No. 4 (winter 1991): 499-533.

Economist Intelligence Unit. *Country Profile: Lebanon, 1996-97.* London: Economist Intelligence Unit, 1997.

Eickelman, Dale. *The Middle East: An Anthropological Approach.* Englewood Cliffs, NJ: Prentice-Hall, 1981.

El-Hashem, Elissa. "Alwailu lahum min Ghadbat Asha'b" (Woe on them From the People's Wrath.) *Nahar Ashabab (al-Nahar* Lebanese daily), Hyde Park, 19 Dec. 1996, p. 25.

Engels, Frederich. *Germany: Revolution and Counter-Revolution.* Trans. L. Krieger. New York: International Publishers, 1937.

Ester, Peter, Loek Halman, and Ruud De Moor, eds. *The Individualizing Society: Value Change in Europe and North America.* Tilburg, the Netherlands: Tilburg University Press, 1993.

Faour, Muhammad. "Pan-Arab Cooperation after Desert Storm.*" Austrian Journal of Development Studies* XI/4 (October 1995): 407-419.

———. *The Arab World After Desert Storm.* Washington, D.C.: United States Institute of Peace, 1993.

———. "The Demography of Lebanon: A Reappraisal.*" Middle Eastern Studies* 27, no. 4 (October 1991): 631-641.

Featherstone, Mike. *Global Culture: Nationalism, Globalization, and Modernity.* Newbury Park, CAL: Sage, 1990.

Fernea, Elizabeth, and Robert Fernea. *The Arab World: Personal Encounters.* Garden City, NY: Anchor Press/Doubleday, 1985.

Frayha, Nemer. "Religious Conflict and the Role of Social Studies for Citizenship Education in the Lebanese Schools Between 1920 and 1983." Ph.D. dissertation, Stanford University, June 1985.

Geis, Florence L. "Self-fulfilling Prophecies: A Social Psychological View of Gender." In *The Psychology of Gender,* ed. Anne E. Beall and Robert J. Sternberg. New York: Guilford Press, 1993.

Giddens, Anthony. *Politics, Sociology and Social Theory.* Stanford, CA: Stanford University Press, 1995.

———. *The Consequences of Modernity.* Cambridge: Polity Press, 1990.

———. *Sociology.* Cambridge: Polity Press, 1989.

———. *The Constitution of Society.* Cambridge: Polity Press, 1984.

————. *New Rules of Sociological Method.* London: Hutchinson, 1976.

Giles Williams, Dorie. "Gender Differences in Interpersonal Relationships and Well-being." *Research in Sociology of Education and Socialization* 5 (1985).

Goode, William J. *The Celebration of Heroes.* Berkeley, CA: University of California Press, 1978.

Habermas, Jurgen. *The Theory of Communicative Action, Vol. Two: The Critique of Functionalist Reason.* London: Heinemann, 1987.

————. *The Theory of Communicative Action, Vol. One: Reason and Rationalization of Society.* London: Heinemann, 1984.

————. *Toward a Rational Society: Student Protest, Science, and Politics.* Trans. Jeremy J. Shapiro. Boston: Beacon Press, 1970.

Hamady, Sonia. *Temperament and Character of the Arabs.* NY: Twayne Publishers, 1960.

Hanf, Theodore. *Coexistence in Wartime Lebanon.* London: Centre for Lebanese Studies, 1993.

————. "Le Comportement Politique des Etudiants Libanais" *Travaux et Jours* 46 (Jan-March, 1973):5-52.

Harding, Stephen, David Phillips, and Michael Fogarty. *Contrasting Values in Western Europe. Unity, Diversity, and Change.* London: MacMillan, 1986.

Harik, Iliya. "Rethinking Civil Society· Pluralism in the Arab World." *Journal of Democracy*, Vol. 5, no. 3 (July 1994): 56.

Harris, William. *Faces of Lebanon* Princeton, NJ: Markus Wiener Publishers, 1997.

Hatab, Zuhayr, and Abbas Makki. *al-Sulta al-Abawiyya Washshabab* (Patriarchy and the Youth). Beirut: Ma'had al-Inma' al-Arabi, 1981.

Hazelrigg, Lawrence. "Individualism." In *Encyclopedia of Sociology*, ed. Edgar F. Borgatta and Marie L. Borgatta. Vol. 2. New York: Macmillan, 1992.

Homans, George. *Social Behavior: Its Elementary Forms*. New York: Harcourt, Brace and World, 1961.

Hourani, Albert. *Syria and Lebanon* London: Oxford University Press, 1954.

Hudson, Michael C. *The Precarious Republic: Political Modernization in Lebanon*. A Westview Encore Edition. Boulder, CO: Westview Press, 1985.

Hui, C.H., and H.C. Triandis. Individualism and Collectivism: A Study of Cross-Cultural Researchers," *Journal of Cross-Cultural Psychology* 17 (1986): 225-248.

Ibn Khaldun, Abdulrahman. *The Muqaddima: an Introduction to History*. Trans. Franz Rosenthal. Princeton, N.J.: Princeton University Press, 1967.

Inglehart, Ronald. *Modernization and Postmodernization: Cultural, Economic, and Political Change in 43 Societies*. Princeton, NJ: Princeton University Press, 1997.

Kahn, Ronald. *Survey of Social Science: Government and Politics Series*. Vol. 4. Ed. Frank N. Magill. Englewood Cliffs, NJ: Salem Press, 1994. Pp. 1402-1403.

Kasser, T.; Ryan, R. M.; Zax, M.; Sameroff, A. J. "The Relations of Maternal and Social Environments To Late Adolescents Materialistic and Prosocial Values." *Developmental Psychology* 31, No. 6 (Nov. 1995): 907-914.

Khalaf, Samir. *Lebanon's Predicament*. New York: Columbia University Press, 1987.

_____. *Reclaiming Beirut*. Beirut: Dar Annahar, 1993.

Khalaf, Samir, and Philip Khoury, eds. *Recovering Beirut: Urban Design and Post-War Reconstruction*. Leiden: Brill, 1993.

Khashan, Hilal. *Inside the Lebanese Confessional Mind*. Lanham, MD: University Press of America, 1992.

_____. "The Political Values of Lebanese Maronite College Students." *Journal of Conflict Resolution*, Vol. 34, No.4 (December 1990): 723.

Khuri, Fuad. *Tents and Pyramids.* London: Saqi Books, 1990.

_____. *Tribe and State in Bahrain.* Chicago: Chicago University Press, 1980.

_____. *From Village to Suburb.* Chicago: Chicago University Press, 1975.

Kidder, Louise H. *Selltiz, Wrightman and Cook's Research Methods in Social Relations*, 4th ed. New York: Holt, Rinehart and Winston, 1981.

Kluckhohn, Clyde. "Values And Value Orientations In The Theory Of Action." In *Toward A General Theory of Action,* ed. Talcott Parsons and Edward A. Shils. New York: Harper and Row, 1951.

Kraus, Stephen J. "Attitudes and the Prediction of Behavior: A Meta-Analysis of the Empirical Literature." *Personality and Social Psychology Bulletin,* 21 (1, 1995): 58-75.

Laroui, Abdullah. *The Concept of the State.* Beirut: Dar al Haqiqa, 1973.

Layder, Derek. *Understanding Social Theory.* London: Sage publications, 1994.

Lebanese Parliament, House of Parliament. "The Lebanese Constitution with all Amendments." Beirut, 1990.

Lebanon, Ministry of Planning. *Enquete Sur La Population Active Au Liban, Novembre 1970.* Beirut: Ministry of Planning.

Lebanon, Ministry of Health. *The Lebanese Survey of Maternal and Child Health 1996.* Beirut: Ministry of Health, 1998.

Lebanon, Ministry of Social Affairs. "The Survey of Housing and Population: Statistical Tables." Beirut: Ministry of Social Affairs, 1996.

Lebanon Family Planning Association. *al-Usra fi Lubnan* (The Family in Lebanon). 2 vols. Beirut: Lebanon Family Planning Association, 1974.

Levinson, Hanna. "Multidimensional Locus of Control in Psychiatric Patients.*" Journal of Consulting and Clinical Psychology* 41, 3 (1973):397-404.

Loeb, Paul Rogat. *Generation at the Crossroads: Apathy and Action on the American Campus.* New Brunswick, N.J.: Rutgers University Press, 1994.

Longrigg, Stephen. *Syria and Lebanon Under the French Mandate.* London: Oxford University Press, 1958.

Lorber, Judith. "Gender." In *Encyclopedia of Sociology*, ed. Edgar F. Borgatta and Marie L. Borgatta. Vol. 2. New York: Macmillan, 1992.

Lott, Bernice, and Diane Maluso. "The Social Learning of Gender." In *The Psychology of Gender,* ed. Anne E. Beall and Robert J. Sternberg. New York: Guilford Press, 1993.

Mansfield, Peter. *The Arabs.* New York: Penguin, 1985.

Marx, Karl, and Frederich Engels. *Selected Works.* London: Lawrence and Wishart, 1968.

Meier, Robert F. "Norms and the Study of Deviance: A Proposed Research Strategy." In *Deviant Behavior: Readings in the Sociology of Norm Violations*, ed. Clifton D. Bryant. New York: Hemisphere Publishing Corporation, 1990.

Melikian, Levon. "Themes in the Personality of Arab Youth." Unpublished manuscript. Beirut: American University of Beirut, no date.

Melikian, Levon, and Lutfy N. Diab. "Stability and Change in Group Affiliations of University Students in the Arab Middle East. " *Journal of Social Psychology* 93 (1974): 13-21.

Merton, Robert. *On Theoretical Sociology: Five Essays, Old and New.* New York, Free Press, 1967.

Nahar Ashabab: Hyde Park. 8 Oct. 1996; 29 Oct. 1996.

Nasr, Nafhat and Monte Palmer. "Alienation and Political Participation in Lebanon," *International Journal of Middle East Studies* 8 (1977): 493-516.

Nisbet, Robert. *Sociological Tradition.* New York: Basic Books, 1966.

Nisbet, Robert, and Robert G. Perrin. *The Social Bond.* 2d ed. New York: Alfred A. Knopf, 1977.

Parsons, Talcott. *The Social System.* New York: Free Press, 1951.

Parsons, Talcott, and Robert F. Bales. *Family Socialization and Interaction Process.* New York: Free Press, 1955.

Patai, Raphael. *The Arab Mind.* Rev. ed. New York: Scribner, 1983.

Random House Compact Unabridged Dictionary. Special 2nd ed. New York: Random House, 1996.

Ritzer, G. *Frontiers of Social Theory:The New Syntheses.* New York: Columbia University Press, 1990.

Rokeach, Milton. *The Nature of Human Values.* New York: The Free Press, 1973.

Rose, G. M.; Shoham, A.; Kahle, L. R.; Batra, R. "Social Values, Conformity, and Dress." *Journal of Applied Social Psychology* 24, no. 17 (Sept. 1994): 1501-1519.

Salibi, Kamal. *A House of Many Mansions: The History of Lebanon Reconsidered.* London: I.B.Tauris & Co, 1988.

Sax, Linda J.; Alex W. Astin; William S Korn; Kathryn M. Mahoney. *The American Freshman: National Norms for Fall 1995.* Los Angeles, CAL: UCLA, 1995.

Schmitter, Philippe. "Society." In *The Transition to Democracy: Proceedings of a Workshop.* National Research Council. Washington, D.C.: National Academy Press, 1991.

Scott, John. *Sociological Theory: Contemporary Debates.* Brookfield, Vermont: Edward Elgar Publishing Company, 1995.

Sharabi, Hisham. *Neopatriarchy: A Theory of Distorted Change in Arab Society.* New York: Oxford University Press, 1988.

Stryker, Sheldon. "Identity Theory." In *Encyclopedia of Sociology,* ed. Edgar F. Borgatta and Marie L. Borgatta. Vol. 2. New York: Macmillan, 1992.

Triandis, Harry C. *Individualism and Collectivism.* Boulder, CO: Westview Press, 1995.

Wallerstein, Immanuel. *The Modern World System.* 3 vols. San Diego: Academic Press, 1974-1988.

————. "Social Science and the Quest for a Just Society." *American Journal of Sociology* 102, no. 5 (March 1997): 1255.

Weber, Max. "Bureaucratic Authority." In *Sociological Writings,* ed. Wolf Heyderbrand and Max Weber and trans. Martin Black with Lance W. Garmer. New York: Continuum, 1994.

Williams, J.E. and D.L. Best. *Measuring Sex Stereotypes: A Thirty Nation Study.* Beverly Hills, CA: Sage, 1982.

Williams, Robin M. Jr. "Change and Stability in Values and Value Systems: A Sociological Perspective." In *Understanding Human Values, Individual And Societal,* ed. Milton Rokeach. New York: The Free Press, 1979.

Yusuf Ali, 'Abdullah. *The Meanings of the Holy Qur'an.* New ed. Brentwood, MD: Amana Corporation, 1993.

Zay'our, Ali. *Tahlil al-Dhat al-Arabiya* (Analysis of the Arab Ego). Beirut: Dar Attali'ah, 1977.

Zuhur, Sherifa. *Revealing Reveiling: Islamist Gender Ideology in Contemporary Egypt.* Albany, NY: State University of New York Press, 1992.

INDEX

Adorno, Theodor, 76
analysis of variance, 9, 34, 69, 156, 157, 158, 159
ANOVA, 9, 70
al-Akhtal al-Saghir, 1
al-Amin, Adnan, 30, 122
al-Hakim, Towfiq, 147
Althusser, Louis, 19
Amal, 60
American University of Beirut, 3, 5 *See* also AUB
anomie, 15, 17
Arab culture, 69, 83, 85
Arab nationalists, 94, 96, 124, 138
Arab society, 23, 85, 90
Arslan, Talal, 61, 119
As'ad clan, 60
attitudes, 2, 5, 7, 8, 13, 20, 21, 22, 28, 33, 41, 76, 107, 109, 114, 119, 125, 129, 138, 141, 142, 143, 144, 146, 149
   political, 3, 4, 29, 30, 113, 152
   social, 14, 29, 135
   and sect, 20, 119, 129, 135, 138, 141, 142, 144
AUB, 3, 5, 6, 8, 28, 31, 34, 35, 36, 37, 38, 39, 40, 70, 74, 77, 78, 79, 80, 81, 82, 83, 84, 85, 86, 90, 91, 92, 94, 95, 96, 98, 99, 100, 101, 102, 103, 104, 105, 106, 107, 108, 111, 113, 114, 115, 116, 118, 119, 120, 121, 122, 123, 124, 125, 126, 127, 128, 129, 130, 131, 132, 133, 134, 135, 136, 137, 138, 139, 140, 141, 142, 145, 146, 147, 150, 166, 175, 181, 182, 184, 188, 190 *See* also American University of Beirut

authoritarianism, 7, 8, 14, 32, 69, 73, 76, 77, 78, 80, 81, 88, 92, 96, 103, 105, 109, 110, 115, 143, 144, 147, 149, 153, 156, 158, 162
authority, 8, 14, 20, 27, 57, 60, 76, 77, 79, 80, 81, 96, 99, 101, 103, 105, 107, 110, 111, 143, 144, 145, 146, 147, 148, 150, 151, 152, 154, 157, 187
Aoun, Michel, 60, 114, 115, 117, 118, 120, 121, 123, 124
Barakat, Halim, 6, 29, 30, 32, 40, 54, 58, 69, 90, 98, 114, 126, 136, 149
Beck, Ulrich, 18, 69
Bell, Daniel, 26
Bellah, Robert, 70
Berri, Nabih, 60
Bourdieu, Pierre, 5, 18, 20, 21
bureaucracy, 53, 56, 59, 65, 67, 131
Catholic, 38, 39, 63, 87, 104, 110, 119, 121, 122, 123, 131, 132, 140, 161, 163, 164, 171, 183, 188
Christians, 6, 38, 40, 43, 55, 56, 58, 61, 62, 66, 103, 109, 117, 118, 126, 139, 141, 163, 164
civil society, 41, 52, 53, 67, 153
civil strife, 1, 43, 58, 81, 90, 120, 141, 147
collectivism, 14, 70, 71, 76, 143, 145
community, 4, 9, 14, 16, 17, 21, 26, 56, 59, 71, 89, 94, 96, 124, 125, 133, 138, 144, 149, 151